Lincolnshire Railways

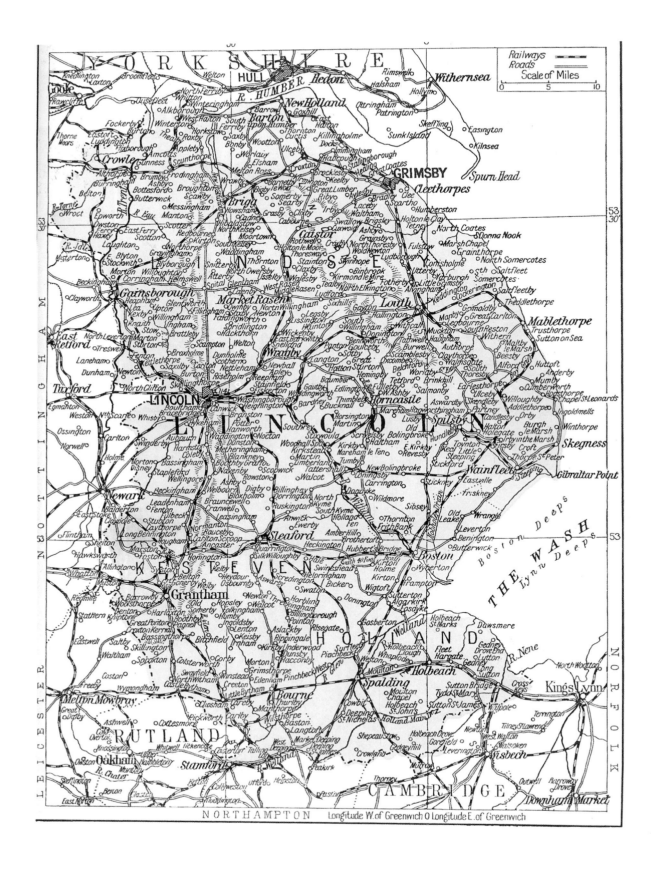

Lincolnshire Railways

ALAN STENNETT

THE CROWOOD PRESS

First published in 2016 by
The Crowood Press Ltd
Ramsbury, Marlborough
Wiltshire SN8 2HR

www.crowood.com

© Alan Stennett 2016

British Library Cataloguing-in-Publication Data
A catalogue record for this book is available from the British Library.

ISBN 978 1 78500 082 9

FRONTISPIECE: Railway map of Lincolnshire in 1920 at the peak of the system. The only lines not shown are the Edenham and Little Bytham Railway and the Alford and Sutton Tramway, both of which closed before the end of the nineteenth century.

All images are from the author's collection unless otherwise stated.

Typeset by Bookcraft Ltd, Stroud, Gloucestershire
Printed and bound in India by Replika Press Pvt. Ltd.

Contents

Introduction and Acknowledgements

It has been a great privilege to be asked to write this description of the railways of Lincolnshire, but it would not have been possible without all the work that has been put in, and continues to be done, by many authors and local railway historians. Large numbers have worked on various local projects but special mention must be made of Alf Ludlam, Stewart Squires, John Rhodes, Stephen Walker, C. T. Goode and the late John Ruddock, whose works have been particularly valuable.

Pictures have come from many sources, and I can only hope that due credit has been given for all those that have been used. I have been particularly grateful to John Foreman, Stuart Ray, Michael Barratt, John Meredith, Graham Lightfoot, M. Cook, Ray Heppenstall, John Fisher, David and John Ford, Brian Rose, Richard Goodman, P. Loftis and Jack Overton or to their friends or families for permission to use some of their original works.

I have also been fortunate to be able to make use of the collections held by David Robinson, Rod Knight, John Musselwhite, Stuart Gibbard, Bryan Longbone and Mrs Scott, as well as for material held in the archives of the National Railway Museum, and of Lincolnshire, North-East Lincolnshire and North Lincolnshire Councils.

Every effort has been made to ensure that copyright material has been approved and acknowledged in this book. Any errors and oversights should be referred to the writer, and will be corrected in later editions

I am very grateful to Rod Knight, Adam Cartwright and Mike Hartley for their efforts to ensure that I have not made too many silly errors, but I should add that any that remain are entirely my responsibility.

I must also thank Sue, my wife, for her tolerance at various times during the writing and compilation of this work and for her continuing interest in railways, despite my not entirely keeping my promise that we would not live in a museum when we moved into Woodhall Junction!

CHAPTER I

Lincolnshire Before the Railways

A Difficult County for Travellers

Communications in Lincolnshire before the railways was a matter of ancient routes and even older waterways. Our main highways still follow the roads that the Romans built two millennia ago, and a county where much of the land was frequently inundated found water transport an invaluable and sometimes essential way to get around.

This historic county has always presented difficulties to the traveller. The large areas of the Fens in the south-east, the Carrs of the Isle of Axholme at the opposite corner, and the marshes along much of the coast were constantly changing areas of mud, water and soggy bits of land, with few easily discernible ways through them. Most land routes, therefore, followed the limestone spine of the Heath and Cliff or the higher lands of the chalk Wolds in the north-east.

The influence of the Romans is very clear. The major north–south route within the county follows parts of Ermine Street, King Street and Mareham Lane from near Peterborough, through Sleaford and Lincoln, to the Humber close to Winteringham. The A46, still the main access to Lincoln from the west, follows the line of the Fosse Way as it strikes diagonally from Newark through Lincoln towards the north-eastern coast. From Lincoln to the coast, the road curves around the northern edge of the

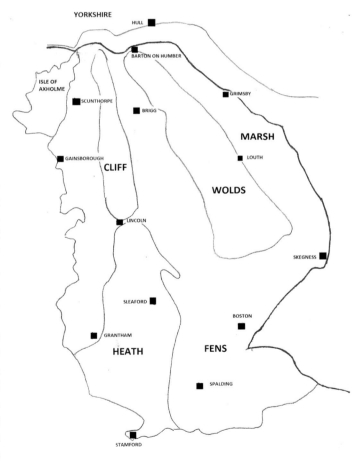

General topography of Lincolnshire.

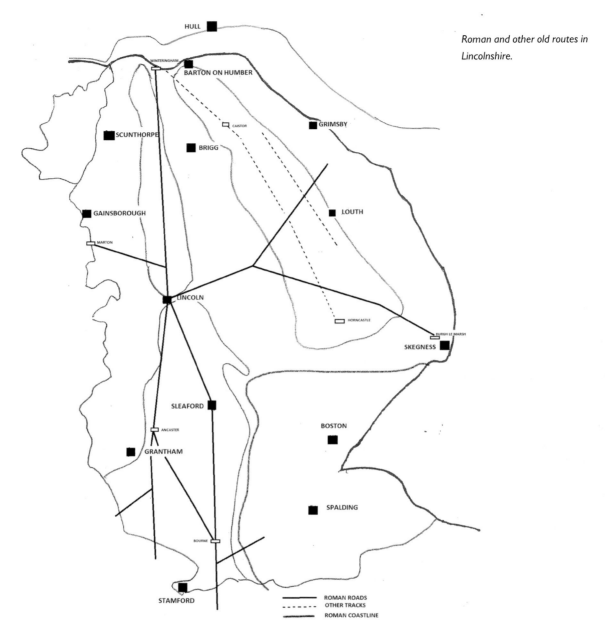

Roman and other old routes in Lincolnshire.

Fens to the Roman Banovallum – Horncastle – then on towards Wainfleet and what may well have been a Roman port, now lost to the sea, near Skegness. Other key routes include Tillbridge Lane, from just north of Lincoln to what was a ford over the Trent at Marton; more of Ermine Street through Ancaster towards Stamford; and the Salt or Salters Way – now the A52 – from near Grantham across the

Bridge End Causeway to Donington, then towards the salt workings on the coast or in the marshes. It may also have served a port in Bicker Haven, then open to the sea.

Many other Roman roads and tracks have been identified, but it is likely that a number of them followed existing Iron Age or earlier track-ways. The Salt Way was almost certainly pre-Roman, and although the arrow-straight line of Ermine Street suggests that it was new in Roman times, it closely follows the older Jurassic Way cliff-edge paths of Middle Street and Pottergate. Caistor High Street, running north from Horncastle to Caistor, is almost certainly pre-Roman, as are the Bluestones Heath Road and Bartongate, along the edge of the Marsh. Mareham Lane could also have been in use before the Roman occupation.

Where the Iron Age salt merchants and the Roman legions failed to penetrate on land, they, and the locals, took to the water. The Witham itself, running north from near Grantham before turning through the Lincoln Gap then south to the Wash, with its tributaries the Slea, the Bain and the Brant, would have been the main water 'highway' into, and around, the county; but the other fenland rivers – Welland, Glen and Nene – remained important routes well into modern times. In the north, the Ancholme, the Trent and the Idle were all significant waterways, but a great deal of water traffic would simply have been along the creeks and lagoons of the Fens and marshes. Lincoln's museum, the Collection, has a fine log boat found in the muds of the Witham, along with records of many similar vessels, and archaeological finds such as the Witham Shield, now in the British Museum, suggest that the waterways of the county had a strong religious significance, as well as facilitating travel in the county.

The Romans also made good use of the waterways, constructing the Foss Dyke linking the Witham at Lincoln and the Trent near Torksey. They are also the most probable diggers of the long cut known as the Carr Dyke, running along the fen edge from near Peterborough to Lincoln. It seems likely this was mainly a catch-water drain, taking water coming off the higher land to prevent it flooding into the Fens, which appear to have been drier in Roman times. It may have been used for transport, but the evidence is scanty. Excavations in Lincoln show it was an important centre for water-borne transport. Bawtry, on the Idle, was also a Roman port; Spalding and Bourne may well have

been, and there seems little doubt that they made good use of the fenland waterways as well.

Doing as the Romans Did

All these options meant that Lincolnshire in about the third or fourth century AD had a reasonably comprehensive network of communications covering much of the county. Unfortunately, that was about where it stopped for the next few hundred years. The old roads remained, although opportunistic locals mined the Roman surfaces for their stone, but very little changed. New fenland routes linked growing settlements on the low ridges of dry land between the marsh and the fen from Spalding through Holbeach to Long Sutton and along the silt ridge from Boston towards Wainfleet. The influence of the landscape is clear from those roads and the path of what is now the A16, running due south from Spilsby to Boston through the 'islands' of Stickney and Sibsey. It follows the line of a glacial moraine, a low ridge of clay and stones marking the furthest limit of the last Ice Age in the area.

Through medieval times the pack-horse and the ox-drawn wagon would have been the main means of land transport in the county. It would probably be fair to say that very few people travelled any distance in what became a region of small market towns, spaced out according to how far it was practical to drive livestock and return within a day.

The rivers remained important, although the lack of central authority saw the Foss Dyke fall into disrepair, the Witham was often unnavigable for long periods and the fenland rivers frequently silted up. Lincoln and Stamford remained as important regional centres, and Boston became a major port, with a hinterland largely served by water transport. It developed an important role in trading wool to the Continent, often produced by the great monastic houses to be found all over Lincolnshire. Other smaller ports along the county's coast thrived in medieval times on trades of fish, salt, peat and other goods, along the English coasts and to the near Continent.

A peat bog on the Isle of Axholme. Much of Lincolnshire would have been similar to this before large-scale drainage. LINCOLNSHIRE WILDLIFE TRUST

The reclamation of the Fens, the Isle of Axholme and the Ancholme Carrs in the seventeenth and eighteenth centuries improved communications there, since many of the new drains were navigable, allowing the transport of goods and people. Agricultural produce was the main traffic, but the rising populations of the Fens in particular saw a demand for packet boats into Boston, as well as market boats – in effect mobile water-borne shops. That traffic continued well into the twentieth century, supplemented in many areas by small-scale producers of commodities like milk, butter and eggs, taking them to the market towns by boat.

Rivers and Canals

The drainage work had the incidental benefit of improving the major rivers for navigation, with the Witham Navigation completed by 1770 and work carried out to improve through passage to the Foss Dyke a few years later. The Trent, the Glen, the Ancholme, the Bourne Eau and the Welland also saw increased use following improvement works.

Canal mania came early to Lincolnshire – the Louth Canal was planned in the 1750s, although it did not reach the town until 1770. The Sleaford Navigation and the Horncastle Canals were opened later in that century, although both were effectively canalized rivers that had been used by boats in the past. The Grantham Canal was a more serious engineering proposition, needing to cut through a ridge between the town and the Trent Valley before dropping steeply down a flight of locks to join the river itself near Nottingham. The Caistor Canal also required significant engineering works, with six locks in its 4-mile (6km) length, which probably accounted for it never reaching its intended terminus on Navigation Lane at Caistor, but petering out at Moortown, 3 miles (4km) away.

Despite that relative failure, the planned role of the canal, as laid out in the following quote from the prospectus, gave a good indication of the thinking behind all of Lincolnshire's waterway projects, and that of most of the railways that followed.

> By this canal, and the Ancholme Navigation, the surplus agricultural produce of the north of Lincolnshire is exported; and coal, agricultural lime, and general merchandise is the return to Caistor and its neighbourhood.

At roughly the same time that the waterways were being upgraded, the same was happening on the roads. The old system of repair under which every local inhabitant was required to spend four days a year working on the roads, providing his own tools and transport, was never going to result in satisfactory surfaces. A partial solution was the introduction of Turnpike Trusts, with repairs paid for by tolls charged to users. Lincolnshire joined the turnpike revolution in 1726, when part of the Great North Road near Grantham was taken, followed a few years later by a further stretch south towards Stamford. Most Lincolnshire turnpikes, however, were established in the second half of the century. Toll bridges were an important part of the process, with Dunham Bridge opened in 1756 over the Trent on the road from Lincoln into Nottinghamshire, followed in 1791 by Gainsborough, also over the Trent, and Tattershall, over the Witham, in 1795. Two other bridges, Fosdyke and Cross Keys, over the Welland and Nene, respectively, were available to travellers by the early years of the next century.

Faster by Road

The new roads not only allowed goods to move more freely, they also permitted speedier travel, with stagecoaches running from Lincoln to London in 1784 and extended to the Humber a few years later. By 1820, a network of coaches covered much of the county, bringing with them some of the best-known inns and hotels to be found in the county.

As the railway age dawned elsewhere in Britain, it could reasonably be claimed that Lincolnshire's communications were very nearly back to being as good as they had been during Roman times, and looked very similar. The system in the Fens was better, and a route across the north of the county, from Gainsborough to Louth by way of Caenby Corner and Market Rasen, was in regular use. Lincoln, Stamford, Grantham, Boston, Spalding, Brigg, Barton-upon-Humber and Gainsborough were well-established centres. Louth had become a more important communication centre, and Grimsby was growing rapidly after action had been taken to clear the Haven and to build new dock facilities.

The Agricultural Revolution had transformed the county's main industry, as draining and enclosures made more land available, and better farming systems saw lower-quality pastures put under the plough for the first time. The need for improved agricultural implements to work that land also drove the Industrial Revolution in the county as small-scale blacksmiths, wheelwrights, tool-makers and foundries diversified into manufacturing what was needed. Wheelwright John Cooke built ploughs in Lincoln; foundryman William Howden of Boston constructed the county's first portable steam engine; millwright James Hart built threshing machines at Brigg; and blacksmith's apprentice

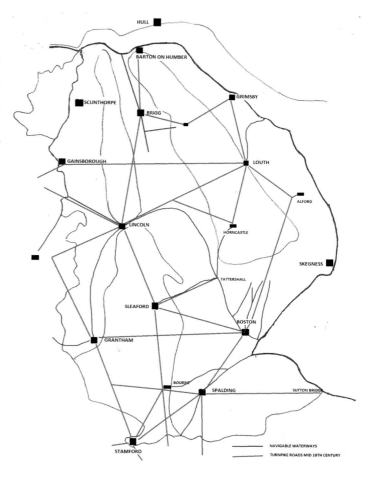

Turnpike roads and navigable waterways by the early 1800s.

Richard Hornsby made an adjustable harrow in his employer's forge near Grantham.

All of these entrepreneurs, and the farming industry that they served, were in need of efficient, reliable transport to bring in raw materials and to take away produce and manufactured items. The county was ready for the railways.

CHAPTER 2

Dreams, Schemes and Competition

Mind the Gap?

Lincolnshire itself was not an obvious early target for railway promoters. The large area and widely distributed populations offered few opportunities to link population centres with passenger services or to develop a substantial flow of goods. The first line that we would now recognize as a railway opened between Stockton and Darlington in 1825, but no trains would run in Lincolnshire for another twenty years. However, one geographical feature in the county did attract a great deal of attention from early promoters, planners and surveyors: the Lincoln Gap, a break in the limestone ridge running north and south through the county, offered a level route for lines from London to the north, and compared favourably with the existing lines by way of Derby and Rugby. As far back as 1821 it had been suggested that the proposed London and Cambridge Railway should be extended to Lincoln and later to York. The proposed route had been surveyed by John and George Rennie in 1827, with trains crossing the Fens on the level, turning west through the Gap, then north up the Trent Valley to Yorkshire.

All but one of the proposals coming from the south made use of the Lincoln Gap, but many alternative ways to it were suggested. The two main options were lines coming over the Fens from the direction of Cambridge, and those, usually by way of Peterborough, that linked to existing lines there and offered the possibility of a faster, more direct, passage to the capital.

Before anyone could start to build a new line, a lengthy process of preparation and parliamentary scrutiny had to be gone through. A company would first be set up to raise enough money to survey the proposed route and assess its commercial prospects. If that was successful a bill was then presented to Parliament to allow the company to be formally established and to give it powers including the right to acquire land by compulsory purchase, cross highways and waterways and establish fair arbitration procedures to settle disputes. At this point, opposition was likely to be met by rival railway or canal companies, private landowners and others affected by the plans. Many projects failed at this stage, but even those that passed were not guaranteed an easy progression. All the restrictions and requirements built into the bill would be closely scrutinized by opponents, who would also be able to object to the modifications to the initial plans that were almost inevitable once the line began to be built. Approval also committed the new company to building the line as proposed; it could not suddenly decide to simply give up without getting parliamentary approval for that, since other parties would be considered to have lost out by any such abandonment.

'Lincoln from the Great Northern Railway' as drawn in 1852 by Rock & Co. of London, incorporating a paddle steamer and some early train spotters. If the perspective is correct, the bridge is probably that of the MS&L line to Grimsby. LINCS TO THE PAST. REF LCL 6692

Even when the line was completed, official-dom had a further role to play, in that an inspector, usually from the Board of Trade, had to pass the works as being fit for purpose. Many schemes, trying to reduce costs and get an income from traffic as quickly as possible, found that their plans were held up by a failed inspection.

The argument about how Lincoln was to be served was long and complicated. Ruddock and Pearson, in their *Railway History of Lincoln* (1985), identified thirty different possibilities, proposals and parliamentary applications between that first suggestion in 1821 and a train actually turning its wheels in the county in the middle 1840s. The principal companies involved included the Grand Northern, rejected by Parliament in 1836, and the Great Northern – not the later successful contender, but another using the name – which also failed to get parliamentary backing. Both would have approached from the Cambridge direction, as would the Northern and Eastern and an early London and York. But, in 1844, the Cambridge and York, origi-nally planned to come from Cambridge by way of Peterborough then through the Fens, changed its

mind and surveyed a line direct from Peterborough to London. It then took the name of the London and York and amalgamated with the Direct Northern, the only company that did not want to pass through the Lincoln Gap, planning instead to take a harder, but faster, run from Peterborough to Grantham, and on through Gainsborough to the north, with branches to Lincoln and Retford.

The combined London & York and Direct Northern companies, taking the name of the Great Northern, then modified its line from Grantham to go on through Newark and Retford to Doncaster, with much of the drive for the change coming from Edmund Denison, the MP for Doncaster, later Chairman of the GNR. This line missed Lincoln and Gainsborough completely, but both were put back on their map after the Lincolnshire Loop Line, by way of Spalding and Boston, was added to their plans. This was achieved by absorbing the proposed Wakefield, Lincoln and Boston Railway, which planned to follow the River Witham between Lincoln and Boston.

The package seemed to offer a combination of advantages, including the fast link to the north; a

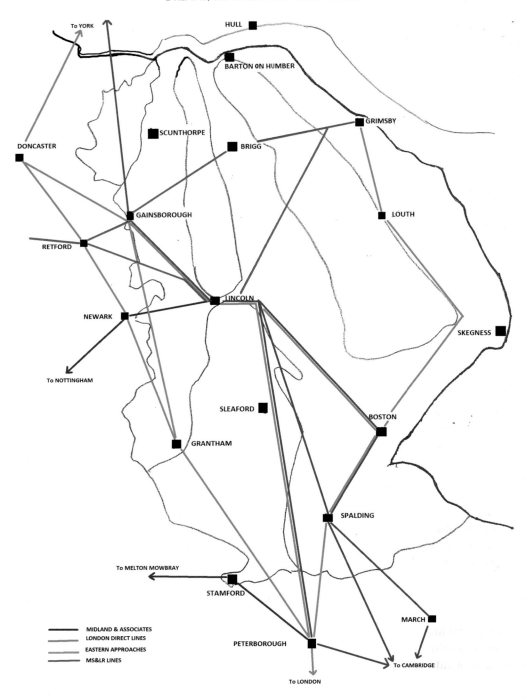

Alternative routes from London to York as planned by 1845. The London Direct routes were all built by 1852, other than the direct Peterborough to Lincoln and Grantham to Gainsborough connections, neither of which were added later. The Eastern approach was later connected from March through Spalding and Sleaford as far as Lincoln with the opening of the Great Northern & Great Eastern Joint Railway in 1882. The direct Lincoln to York connection, avoiding Doncaster, was never built. MS&L lines and the East Lincolnshire Railway are also shown. The MS&L Gainsborough to Retford tracks were used by the Great Northern before the Gainsborough to Doncaster section was completed as part of the Joint.

relatively direct, albeit slow, route from Lincoln to London; the possibility of some early earnings from the easily built Loop Line and a block to proposals by the Eastern Counties. However, the battle for Lincoln was not yet over.

The Railway King Takes an Interest

The Midland Railway, or, perhaps more to the point, its chairman, George Hudson, known as the Railway King, was determined that a rival, faster, route to York, other than that offered by companies he controlled, should not be established. Hudson was also chairman of the Eastern Counties Railway and became one of the key drivers of that route option. Back in the 1830s, the Midland Counties Railway, one of the founding companies of the Midland, had proposed a line from Lincoln to their own line at Nottingham. Another possibility was the Swinton, Doncaster and Lincoln Railway, linking the city with lines to Doncaster and into Yorkshire. Proposed in 1844, it was intended to connect to lines south of the city, either by way of Ely, Wisbech and Boston or through St Ives and Peterborough – a proposal that only failed to receive parliamentary approval because of errors in the documentation submitted to the House of Commons.

The chaotic situation in Parliament, with a large number of bills presented in 1844, all proposing variations on much the same theme, led to the setting up of an inquiry by the Board of Trade. Given the task of considering 'the schemes for extending railway communication between London and York', it quickly decided that there was a need for such improvement. It threw out the Midland's ideas as being too circuitous, and felt that the Towns Line would be too expensive to build, but failed to back one single project from among the other possibilities. It did recommend that the line to Lincoln by way of Cambridge was the best option for the southern section, but then backed the Direct Northern's plans north of the city, by way of Gainsborough, which had already been rejected by Parliament.

Confusion in Lincoln

The City of Lincoln itself had taken an active part in these discussions. A committee there had looked at all the proposals as they stood in the middle 1830s, and had come down, not surprisingly, in favour of a direct route to London, rather than cutting across to the Midlands. They backed the Grand Northern, rather than the first Great Northern, although they felt the Grand Northern's overall plans were too ambitious. Ironically, the City Corporation then backed the Great Northern scheme in Parliament, but to no avail when the bill was thrown out.

Interest was renewed in the 1840s as the options became clearer. Meetings in Lincoln considered the merits of the various cases, including arguments that local traders would find more benefit from the Wakefield–Lincoln–Boston–Peterborough Line than from one to the capital, since coal could be brought in more cheaply from Yorkshire and local livestock farmers could cut the cost of taking animals to that county by between 30 and 50 per cent. To appreciate those benefits, it is estimated that Lincoln received 70,000 tons of coal a year and 20,000 tons of agricultural commodities, such as fertilizer and animal feed, while over 100,000 head of livestock could be expected to head in the opposite direction. The benefits to other parts of the county could be expected to be even greater, since Lincoln was served by the Fossdyke Canal, enabling bulk commodities to be transported more easily than by road. As the London and York pointed out in its 1844 prospectus, this 'most extensive and richly agricultural district in England' stood to gain 'daily opportunities of sending their fat cattle in a few hours' to markets 'without the great loss in weight and value ... by travelling for days together on a turnpike road', as well as offering facilities 'for the shipment of grain, malt and flour, cattle and wool, into the manufacturing districts of Yorkshire and Lancashire'.

The publication of the Board of Trade report in March 1845 set off another round of meetings and speculation. The towns that looked likely to lose out if the recommendations were followed made their views known, and three gatherings were held in Lincoln. The first, organized by groups in favour of the lines supported by the report, saw more than a thousand people, mostly from the City, turn out to vote in their favour. This was followed a few days later by a public meeting, attended by large groups who travelled from all over the area by horse, foot, coach and river-packet to meet in the Castle Yard. This second meeting was a public affair, with supporters from both sides present – the *Doncaster, Nottingham and Lincoln Gazette* described 'twelve stage-coaches, each with four horses', as well as 'thirteen vehicles, each having a pair, and some three, horses' setting out from Newark to support the direct line, while three packet-boats from Boston came to ensure their town was served.

A noisy meeting 'much interrupted by loud outbursts of cheering and hooting' as well as accusations that half-crown (12½p) bribes had been paid to attend, saw numbers of votes taken with no conclusive answer. A result was only achieved when a delayed boat-load of 300 persons from Boston arrived to swing the decision in favour of the London and York/Great Northern proposals to build both the Towns Line and the Lincolnshire Loop. A third session, moved from the Guildhall to the cattle market because of the numbers present, first removed the Mayor from the chair on the grounds of his perceived support for the London and York, then declared unanimous support for the Cambridge Line. The meeting then broke up in what was variously described as 'disorder', 'chaos' and 'a riot'. The Lincoln Town Council then declared that the meeting had been closed when the Mayor was removed from the chair, that the resolution was therefore void, and they backed the Great Northern. When the deputation from Grantham – 'nearly 500 strong' – got back that night , they were met by 'the cheers of the assembled crowds that waited to greet them'.

Parliament Plays its Part

The arguments then moved on to Parliament, which duly threw out all the plans in the 1845 session, with diligent and determined opposition from supporters of George Hudson a key element in the failures. Opposition was not due solely to the empire-building plans of Hudson and his colleagues – there were major financial considerations for individual shareholders. A London merchant, Henry Bruce appears in *The Times* in 1845, having petitioned the House of Commons against the London and York Railway, alleging that £500,000 of its £5,000,000 investment was fraudulent. In his later will he left over £35,000 in Eastern Counties (Cambridge and Lincoln) stock, which would presumably have been of much greater value if the line had been built.

The financial arguments continued into 1845 alongside the political ones. An offer by Eastern Counties shareholders to those of the London and York if they dropped their plans was not taken up, nor was a proposal to merge the two. A merger did take place, though, between the Direct Northern and the London and York as the Great Northern Railway, which received its royal assent in June 1846. Also approved was a partner company, the East Lincolnshire Railway, running from a junction with the GNR at Boston up the east side of the county, linking Alford, Louth and Grimsby. The news caused the Newark bells to be rung in celebration, while in Lincoln 'a grand display of fireworks is to be exhibited in the market-place' and 'in the evening the Montgolfier balloon to ascend' – one hopes not in the vicinity of the fireworks!

The Midland Gets In First

Newark would also have been pleased to hear that another line would be passing through their town, since the Midland Railway had obtained parliamentary approval for its line from Nottingham to Lincoln by way of Newark. The same company had also gained approval for a line from Syston in Leicestershire, on the company's main line, to Peterborough, passing through Stamford. The distance actually travelled in Lincolnshire was small, but it did give the town bragging rights as being the first in the county to be served by a railway. A section of the line from Peterborough to a temporary

The Midland station at Stamford, looking east. The first services in the county began from just beyond the tunnel in the distance. D.N. ROBINSON

station opened for traffic in July 1846, beating the same company's service into Lincoln, which did not start until 4 August.

Rails to Grimsby

Although the north–south routes through the county attracted most of the early attention, other companies were laying their plans to serve the county. In the north, a new grouping was being established to link the port of Grimsby with the industrial areas to the west of Lincolnshire. The old-established Grimsby Haven Company, which became the Grimsby Docks Company in 1845, wanted to be able to find markets for the catch from rich new fishing grounds being established in the North Sea. They promoted the Great Grimsby and Sheffield Junction Railway (GG&SJR) to link the town with New Holland and Gainsborough. Another line, the Sheffield and Lincolnshire Junction Railway (S&LJR), would extend the GG&SJR from Gainsborough to join a third, and longer-established line, the Sheffield, Ashton-under-Lyne and Manchester Railway. Although the three were nominally independent companies, all were well represented on each other's boards and they merged to create the Manchester, Sheffield and Lincolnshire Railway (MS&LR) in 1847. Although

Hull did not appear in any of the various titles, it was obviously intended to be a target market, since the GG&SJR planned to run to New Holland and buy the ferry service from there to Hull. The ferries and the Grimsby Docks Company all became part of the MS&LR.

Other ideas for lines to serve Grimsby or Hull by way of the north of Lincolnshire had been proposed. They included the Manchester, Midland and Great Grimsby Junction; the Hull, Lincoln and Nottingham; the Northampton, Lincoln and Hull Direct; the Derby, Gainsborough and Great

Cancelled share certificate for the Great Grimsby and Sheffield Junction Railway Company.

WHO PAID THE FERRYMEN?

THE NEW HOLLAND FERRY, ON THE HUMBER, BELONGING TO THE MANCHESTER, SHEFFIELD, AND LINCOLNSHIRE RAILWAY.

The MS&L New Holland Ferry. ILLUSTRATED LONDON NEWS

Although the GG&SJR planned to take over the New Holland ferries, they would not be able to do so until their company gained parliamentary approval. Rumours began to circulate that another railway company, operating on the north bank of the Humber, was looking to buy the boats, properties and legal rights, so a group of members of the railway committee purchased the business under their own names for £10,000. According to a newspaper report at the time, this was on behalf of the railway, but when it came to a transfer, the new owners charged themselves as a railway committee the dramatically increased sum of £21,000. A nice little earner, as one might say today, but the deal came back to bite the perpetrators later, when other shareholders became suspicious of a number of deals done in the early days. The board was reorganized to the detriment of the ferry group, and some of them had to pay back part of their profits.

Grimsby Junction and the Lincoln and Great Grimsby, all of which failed to attract sufficient support nationally or locally. One scheme that might have thrived was the Gainsborough and Hull Railway, but the MS&LR group disposed of that potential rival by buying off the promoters with a payment of £6,000.

It may seem surprising that the industrial centre of Scunthorpe did not feature on these early railway plans, but up to the 1860s it was just one of a group of small villages that occupied the site of the present town. It wasn't until the rediscovery of iron ore – our friends the Romans had known about it 2,000 years earlier! – that the development of the Scunthorpe

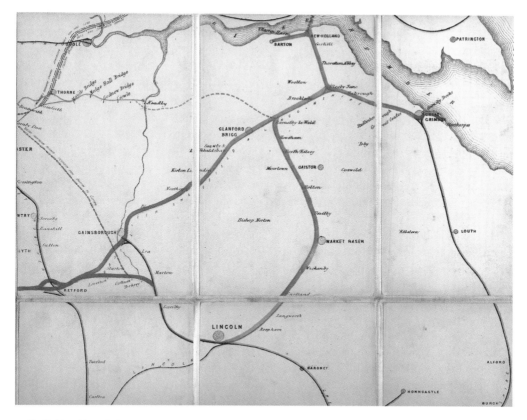

Manchester, Sheffield and Lincolnshire Railway lines in Lincolnshire in 1850.

we know now occurred. It is interesting to speculate as to whether the decisions on the routes to the north might have been different if the town had been as significant in the 1840s as it became later in the nineteenth century.

The main line of the GG&SJR through Brigg to Gainsborough received royal assent in 1845, along with a branch to Market Rasen, which was approved for extension to Lincoln the following year. The Sheffield and Lincolnshire Junction Railway had also promoted the Sheffield and Lincolnshire Extension Railway from their line at Clarborough in Nottinghamshire to cross the Trent at Torksey and continue into Lincoln. That line was also approved.

The first board meeting of the amalgamated Manchester, Sheffield and Lincolnshire Railway

took place on 6 January 1847, and work on the line began almost immediately.

More Ways to Boston

In the north of the county, the Humber was the principal block to lines that might have gone beyond its south bank, although one project, in 1872, did envisage tunnelling under the estuary, but that was thrown out by Parliament on the grounds of 'engineering difficulties'. The result was that lines to Grimsby, in particular, approached the town from the south and, eventually, the west, but not from the north. Further south, Boston, the second-largest town in the county, featured in the plans of a large number of lines, but few saw the town itself as a primary objective. This concerned the merchants and traders of the port, which had a well-established North Sea and Baltic trade going back to the days of the Hanseatic League. To them, the Midlands were the prime objective – as one line proposal put it 'Boston was the closest port to Birmingham – offering return cargoes of manufactured goods or of coal from the Nottinghamshire and Leicestershire mines to the ship owners bringing in timber and other goods from Germany and Scandinavia'.

The town had declared its intention to only support lines that terminated 'as near as possible to the centre of the borough ... and to oppose to the uttermost all others avoiding the town'. Branches of the Cambridge and Lincoln to Boston and Sleaford could have connected to one from the Newark and Sheffield Railway, while the Eastern Counties wanted links to Boston, but neither offered guarantees of transportation further west than Sleaford or Market Deeping. The Boston, Stamford and Birmingham Railway was approved by Parliament, but decided that they would only build the section from Stamford to Wisbech, then failed to carry that through.

Of all the options put forward, only the Ambergate, Nottingham and Boston and Eastern Junction Railway set out to do just what Boston wanted. Planned to serve Grantham, Sleaford and Spalding, in addition to Nottingham and Boston, the Ambergate bought out rival promoters with its own shares. It also took control of the Grantham and Nottingham Canals – a frequent move by railways companies that reduced the parliamentary opposition likely from waterway owners, as well as preventing a rail versus water fares battle breaking out. The same fate was suffered by the Witham and Fossdyke Navigations at the hands of the Great Northern, and the Louth Navigation by the East Lincolnshire; but it usually proved to be beneficial to the canal owners who received a payment in cash or railway shares. Where a waterway was in competition with a railway, as in the case of the Horncastle Canal, financial collapse usually followed.

Many other lines were proposed for Lincolnshire during the 1840s railway mania, but most failed either at the planning stage or in Parliament. Some, such as the 'Bridge-End, Burton Pedwardine, Scredington, Three Queens and Midland Junction Railway', which 'Messrs Bubble and Squeak of Scredington and Mr Timothy Teazer from Burton Pedwardine' put forward in the *Stamford Mercury*, were never intended to be taken seriously in the first place! More lines would be coming to the county, but all would depend on connections with, or support from, lines that had already passed those hurdles, and these will be dealt with later. By 1846, the lawyers, bankers and surveyors had done their job – as had more than a few hucksters and swindlers – but a route map for the first tranche of railways in Lincolnshire was complete. It was now time for the engineers and the builders to take over.

CHAPTER 3

The Builders Arrive

Who Were the Workers?

Railway building in the 1840s was a high-manpower business. Most of the work was done by men with picks and shovels, helped where necessary by blasting techniques based on 1,500-year-old Chinese gunpowder technology. A select group of professional engineers and surveyors were supported by craftsmen such as carpenters, blacksmiths, masons and bricklayers, in turn backed up by gangs of labourers. These could be brought in from outside, but were more often local land-workers enticed away by better rates of pay, albeit at greater risk of injury or even death. It was a substantial army of workers – it has been estimated that, at the height of the railway-building boom of the 1840s, about 200,000 men were building railways, rather more than the total British armed forces at the time. Like those forces, it had its own hierarchy.

At the tip of the pyramid were the engineers, often independent consultants, who determined the general route, helped put the bill through Parliament, then oversaw the actual construction. The role of a railway engineer was relatively new, with many of the early practitioners self-taught or coming from areas such as mining, the military or architectural practice.

Next in line, and overlapping to a certain extent, since many engineers also surveyed 'their' lines, would have been the working surveyors, who took their theodolites, measuring chains and other equipment into the field to plan the details of the route. Bad weather and difficult conditions would have been an accepted occupational hazard for these men, but they also frequently faced irate landowners determined not to have the railway cross their properties. Surveying equipment was damaged, markers removed and physical force employed to deter the intruders. The problem for the surveyors was that, although Parliament required a survey to be done before the bill was presented, it did not give the surveyors the rights to go onto private land to carry it out.

The Sacred Rights of Private Property

Such unwarranted intrusions were deeply regretted by Colonel Charles de Laet Waldo Sibthorp, the MP for Lincoln, who disliked railways in general and the presence of surveyors in particular. He stated in Parliament that he 'had felt it his duty always to stand in opposition to every proposition of every railroad whatever'. He felt government should 'take all possible precautions against the gross attacks and inroads that were made upon that which, until railways were introduced, had been always held sacred – the rights of private property'.

Workmen constructing an embankment on the Midland and Great Northern Railway west of Bourne. FROM 'BUILDING A RAILWAY', BY STEWART SQUIRES AND KEN HOLLAMBY

Fortunately for the Lincolnshire promoters, the local landowners were less outraged than Col. Sibthorp. The principal aristocratic landowner of the north, the Earl of Yarborough, was a strong supporter of the lines that became the MS&LR, and his counterpart in the south, the Earl of Ancaster, actually built his own railway, the Edenham and Little Bytham. The Great Northern had already bypassed much potential opposition by taking control of the Witham and Fossdyke Navigations and building the Lincolnshire Loop Line on their banks. However, one surveyor on the Nottinghamshire/Yorkshire border did report being horse-whipped by an irate Master of Fox Hounds, distressed by the prospect of a railway across his hunting country.

The GNR had more of a problem with landowners' avarice than their opposition – Boston ironfoundry owner William Howden asked £10,000 for land previously valued at £100. The company's solicitor described their 'acuteness at wringing out money from a railway company' as being 'beyond anything he could conceive'. Faced with these claims, it finally took some of the owners to court, which reduced their demands for a total of £27,000 to slightly less than the £12,000 the company had offered. They also had to pay up in a dispute with Councillor Holliday William Hartley, who owned a house and a brewery on the riverbank in Boston. The company had failed to get approval for a modified line through fields partly owned by Cllr Hartley, so had built a single track line along the riverbank, which they owned, but which passed through his gardens to within a yard of his front door. This allowed them to open the line, despite the fact that four tracks converged into one at that point, but Cllr Hartley and a neighbour took them to court and won substantial damages.

Once the surveyors had done their work, the builders could get on with the job. Most railway lines were built by contractors. Some ran large national organizations, building on experience from earlier lines. Among them were Samuel Morton Peto and Edward Ladd Betts, who dealt with the Lincolnshire Loop. The difficult section of the Towns Line near Grantham, with its tunnels, was contracted to Thomas Jackson, who had had experience in working on the Woodhead tunnels in the Pennines. Much of the MS&LR was constructed by John Stephenson & Co., but other lines were built by smaller operators, some of whom only worked on parts of the line. John Waring and Son, from Rotherham, built the Louth-to-Grimsby section of the East Lincolnshire, but gave up the contract for the section between Louth and Boston to Peto and Betts. The engineer of the Ambergate and Boston line was a John Underwood, but the section closest to Grantham was built by John Withers, who came from near Syston, in the neighbouring county of Leicestershire.

Navvies or Not?

The men who actually dug the cuttings, built the embankments and laid the tracks are sometimes known as navvies, short for navigators – the people who dug the canals, or navigations, that preceded the railways – but it would probably be fairer to reserve that title for the ones who made a career of following railway construction around the country. The large majority were people from relatively close by who found railway work more reliable and profitable, although one contractor is recorded as being distressed during harvest time, when many of his workers left to go back to the fields, at least until the opportunities for farming overtime had passed. At the peak of construction in the late 1840s, there would have been several thousand men employed by the companies and the contractors. At Boston over 1,400 were at work on the Loop Line alone in early 1848, with more working on the East Lincolnshire Line. Just under 2,000 were employed on the GNR in the vicinity of Grantham in 1851, under the control of fifteen subcontractors.

Many brought families with them, and most lived in accommodation provided for them by the contractors. In the towns and larger villages, houses were rented. Single men usually lived together in groups, while men with families had a house, but took in lodgers to the limit of the accommodation. In country areas, huts were erected, or workers were lodged on farms with their employees. Samuel Peto had a policy of building barracks with a married man in charge, whose wife cooked for the whole group. He was also concerned about the moral state of his workers. He, or possibly his wife, had a building converted into a chapel, with 'a missionary employed among the workmen during the week, and on the Sabbath he performs service at Gainsborough and Marton'.

Of those 2,000 men at Grantham, three-quarters were described as railway labourers. Brick-makers, bricklayers and their labourers made up the next largest category, with 110 in total. There were 75 miners, which was probably higher than for most Lincolnshire lines, since the section included the tunnels close to the town; 34 blacksmiths, 18 carpenters and 12 masons. The contractors' department employed a total of 41, and there were 14 inspectors and 2 policemen, a tiny number to try to maintain order in such a large body of workers.

About a quarter of the workforce were listed on the 1851 census as having been born in Lincolnshire, but that may not reflect the full total of locally recruited staff, since Nottinghamshire, Leicestershire and Rutland are all as close as, or closer than, some of the fenland locations from where the Lincolnshire men came. Most were farmworkers, who would have earned about ten shillings a week on the land, but could make half that in a single day on the railways.

Navvy housing close to the site of Edmondthorpe and Wymondham station on the Bourne to Saxby section of the Midland and Great Northern Joint Railway which crossed south Lincolnshire. A Navvy Mission was based at the same location to cater for the spiritual needs of the workers. FROM 'BUILDING A RAILWAY', BY STEWART SQUIRES AND KEN HOLLAMBY

The Demon Drink

Railway workers were not usually welcomed in established settlements, although local public houses did well out of their business. Their reputations went ahead of them, although opinions could be very varied. One railway engineer described them as having 'all the daring recklessness of the smuggler, without any of his redeeming qualities', while a local minister felt they were the finest men he had ever seen. They worked hard and sometimes played hard. There are very few recorded cases of major disturbances in Lincolnshire, partly, according to contemporary sources, because the companies stopped paying wages in the local pub. Fights did occur, though, both between the workers and between them and locals. The *Lincolnshire Chronicle* reported that, after the North Thoresby Feast – an annual celebration in Lincolnshire villages – 'a great number of farmers' servants' took on 'a considerable number of workmen on the East Lincolnshire Railway' in 'a most fearful disturbance'. 'Stakes and bludgeons' were used, but no lives were lost and, possibly conveniently, 'the night being dark prevented the constabulary from recognising friend from foe', so no charges were brought. A similar lack of witnesses prevented any action being taken about a brawl between railway men in Grantham that started from an argument about who won a fight between two of them.

In Brigg in 1849, the Riot Act was read to disperse railway navvies and the local stocks were used to punish one of them. Railway workers near the town, at Kettleby, were reported to have broken open coffins in an old cemetery hoping to find coins buried with the dead.

Disputes between workers and contractors could also get violent. At Boston, a Mr Wolds tried to avoid making payment to fourteen labourers, who cornered him in a pub and took him outside to teach him a lesson. At that point they were in turn set upon by thirty other men, presumably in the pay of their intended target, who 'beat them unmercifully'. At Grantham, a similar dispute led to troops being called in. They stopped the fighting, but then got drunk themselves, and had to be sent back on foot, leading their horses, to the barracks in Nottingham.

Getting to Work

The first lines to be built in Lincolnshire were those of the Midland Railway, with its short stretch in Stamford and what was described as 'a rural exploration ... of mostly straight and level pegging' from Newark to Lincoln. Built by Messrs Robert Stephenson and Swanwick, it crossed the county border east of Collingham and arrived at Lincoln St Mark's station by way of Swinderby, Thorpe on the Hill and Hykeham. The intermediate stations were neat, brick-built structures varying from 'Italianate-with-Greek columns' at Collingham to a more basic structure at Hykeham, with staggered platforms surrounded by industrial developments.

St Mark's itself was a substantial building in Greek style, with an Ionic portico in the middle of the north side and Doric columns at the ends. An overall roof of 'strong unpolished glass' covered the platforms, providing 'excellent light' by day, while gas 'splendidly lit' it by night. It was built as a terminus, butting up to Lincoln High Street, but within a few years the MS&LR came in from the east to meet it, creating one of the level-crossings that have bedevilled Lincoln to this day. The station

MS&L/Great Central workmen or contractors for the company working on a bridge at Thorne South on the Scunthorpe to Doncaster line.

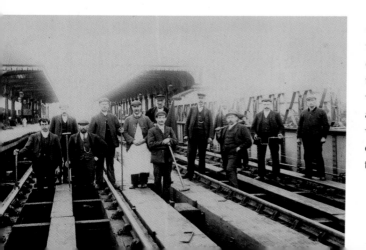

The elaborate Midland station at Collingham, now a private house, although the station remains open.

CHAMPAGNE AND CANNONS

The opening from Nottingham to Lincoln was celebrated by running two trains from key points in the Midland system – Derby and Leicester. The train from the headquarters of the system comprised thirty-five first-class carriages and carried Chairman George Hudson, while that from Leicester was smaller at a mere sixteen vehicles. The two excursions steamed to Lincoln, where champagne and light refreshments were taken and a cannon was fired. Unfortunately, the cannon exploded, fatally injuring its operator, one Paul Harding, who apparently overdid the gunpowder, then crammed the barrel with stones and soil. One onlooker commented that if the cannon had worked correctly, the casualties would probably have been higher!

After the 'light refreshments', the trains returned as far as Nottingham, where 'a large champagne lunch' was taken in the engine shed. In case anyone was still hungry, the trains then went back to Lincoln for a dinner in the evening. They were lucky to have achieved all that travelling without incident, since, two days later, the heavy rain that accompanied the celebrations, and continued afterwards, weakened an embankment causing a locomotive to leave the rails and fall into a drain, killing the fireman. It was suggested later that the frequent passage of such large trains before the embankments had settled properly may have contributed to the accident.

The portico of St Mark's station in Lincoln, still impressive more than a century after first opening. JOHN BARRATT

was provided with goods and passenger facilities, as well as an engine shed to service the locomotives. The line opened on 3 August 1846, giving Lincolnshire its first opportunity to celebrate the arrival of a railway line.

Countywide Construction

Work began in the north of Lincolnshire in late 1845, when the Great Grimsby and Sheffield Junction Railway started its line from Grimsby to Gainsborough. The line, running across the grain of the county, had more difficult terrain to cross that those further south, and three options were considered. The shortest was by way of Caistor, the longest through Market Rasen, but the one selected passed through Brigg and Kirton Lindsey. A branch to Market Rasen was approved, but although other plans were proposed to bring Caistor into the railway age, none were ever built. The main line required a tunnel to be dug at Kirton Lindsey and earthworks were needed near Gainsborough and round the north end of the Wolds. They also had to cross the Trent, but we will come back to that problem later.

With the rush of parliamentary approvals in 1846, several lines began construction almost simultaneously in the county. Most of the companies started work at several locations to get at least part of the system open for traffic, and earning revenue, as soon as possible. Lincolnshire being relatively flat, big earthworks were uncommon and work proceeded swiftly.

The Loop Line ran almost dead straight and level across the Fens to Spalding and Boston before joining the banks of the River Witham to make a more tortuous, but very level, passage to Lincoln. From there it again followed the level banks of a waterway, the Fossdyke, towards Gainsborough, although it did need to cut through a low ridge just before the town. The East Lincolnshire had it even easier – flat across the Fens and the Marsh to join the MS&LR just short of Grimsby, with two of the longest straight stretches to be found on any British railway line. All the Lincolnshire lines crossed

The MS&L station at Gainsborough, later Gainsborough Central. The station was also used by the GN until they built their own at Lea Road. LINCS TO THE PAST, REF LCL 4952

significant numbers of waterways large and small, with the Witham and the Trent requiring substantial bridges to be built – several times in the case of the Witham and, eventually, four for the Trent.

Construction basically started by levelling the ground. Trees and undergrowth would be removed, along with any houses or building unfortunate enough to be in the way of the rails. Where cuttings, embankments and tunnels were needed, 'cut and fill' was used – rock and soil excavated from one location was sent to build raised earthworks at another. Horses pulled wagons full from the diggings to the construction site, picking up speed as they approached the end of the line. Then, just short of the point at which the embankment was being built, and without stopping, the tow lines were unhitched. The wagon ran on and hit a block at the end of the line, tipping its load down to the workmen waiting to spread it where it was needed. The casualty rate among the tip boys, who did the unhitching, was high, and the men below were at risk from falling rocks or by the wagon itself overshooting the block and falling on them. Those were only a few of the ways that men could be killed or injured while at work. Cuttings were excavated by digging away on both sides, then undermining the block in the centre until it collapsed and could be carted away. Predicting the moment of collapse

THE LINE AT SPALDING.

'Straight and level' near Spalding. ILLUSTRATED LONDON NEWS

was an uncertain science and men could easily be trapped. People got run over by contractors' wagons, fell into rivers, got blown up by gunpowder or, like William Codd, got crushed by a 700lb (300kg) rock falling from a cutting face. (It is not recorded who took the trouble to weigh the rock.)

Bridges and culverts were always going to play a big part in the Lincolnshire lines, especially those that crossed drained or reclaimed land, where waterways were very common. The parliamentary bill for the Ambergate railway from Nottingham to Boston included no less than twenty-one clauses relating to the crossing of Deeping Fen and the obligations to the Black Sluice Commissioners, who were responsible for the drainage of an area of land to the west of Boston. The railways had to maintain the banks, ensure that water traffic could pass unhindered, clear ice that built up around bridges,

refrain from modifying the drainage pattern, pay the drainage rates and reinstate any banks or towpaths to 'as good a condition as they were' within twelve months. All of that was to be achieved without in any way diminishing 'the Rights, Powers or Authorities' of the existing 'Undertakers, Adventurers or Participants, Bodies or Persons' in those areas.

Culverts, at this early stage, were usually of brick or stone, with larger bridges of the same materials plus iron and, in the case of the GNR Loop Line in particular, timber. Most of the major bridges on the

Excavating the cutting east of Toft Tunnel near Bourne on the Midland and Great Northern. FROM 'BUILDING A RAILWAY', BY STEWART SQUIRES AND KEN HOLLAMBY

The first Bardney Bridge, on the GN Lincolnshire Loop Line. LINCS TO THE PAST, REF LCL 18829

Loop were built of timber brought into Boston by sea from Scandinavia. The largest were the Grand Sluice Bridge in Boston and the Horsley Deeps Bridge near Bardney, both over the River Witham. The latter, at 729yd (660m), was the longest timber bridge to be built by the GNR, and remained in place until 1860, although a fire on a similar, but smaller structure over the South Forty Foot Drain caused the company to station a watchman at Bardney and probably contributed to their later decision to replace timber with iron on all their bridges.

Boston Bridge Confusion

The bridge at Boston was a cause of some delay in the building of the line, and was one reason why it started later there than elsewhere, despite the fact that much of the timber and iron needed for the building was being brought into the port. The Witham is tidal up to the Grand Sluice, a set of gates built in 1766 to help control drainage and reduce the flood risk. Both the GNR and the East Lincolnshire Railway (ELR) had bridges in their Acts, and both had plans for station location. The ELR intended to cross the river from the east and curve round to a terminus close to the dockside, while the GNR wanted a through station a little way to the west. The costs of duplicating the bridges and stations resulted in a decision to use one bridge and one station as per the GNR's plans, with the ELR line to the docks reduced to a siding, which was not eventually built. The GNR's bridge crossed the Navigation upstream of the sluice, but the combined companies tried to get the plans modified to allow them to cross the tidal section below it. This could have allowed them to avoid incorporating a swing or lifting section into the structure. The Admiralty, who had responsibility for the tidal section, refused to agree to the change, so the bridge was built according to the GNR's specifications alongside and just above the sluice. A movable section was never included, and the bridge crossed the river at a skew, rather than straight across, but neither modification appears to have been taken up by any responsible body. All of these delays contributed to the slow start on construction around Boston.

Building on the banks of the River Witham offered attractive views to travellers. A class 114 diesel multiple unit leaves Bardney for Lincoln in the 1960s. J. FORD, COURTESY DAVID FORD

Apart from those difficulties, both the north–south lines made rapid progress. With the trackbed levelled and the bridges in place, the final stage, laying the track itself, could be completed. The rails were spiked onto timber sleepers before being packed down with ballast, and the materials required had been streaming into Boston, Grimsby, Gainsborough, Louth and other locations ever since the contracts had been placed. Ironically, the trade through some ports, such as Gainsborough, was a final flowering of business before the railway itself took much of it away, although for Grimsby the arrival of the railways was to be the greatest possible boon to its maritime business. The Witham Navigation saw a similar temporary benefit in business, with seven boats carrying pig iron to Lincoln for casting into rail spikes and fittings.

Knowledge of who was going to get the contracts for the East Lincolnshire Railway must have been revealed before they were signed, since work started in several locations before the formal dates. According to the *Lincoln and Stamford Mercury* 'excavation and levelling' was taking place near Grimsby in early December 1846, with work 'progressing rapidly' at two other points the following month; sixty to seventy men and twenty tip-wagons were at work, temporary rails laid and brick-makers preparing materials for bridges.

The GNR ordered 30,000 tons of wrought iron rails and 350,000 fir sleepers in November 1846, and work was going on at Lincoln and Gainsborough, and on the banks of the Witham, before the end of the year. The *Nottingham Journal* noted that buildings on the High Street in Lincoln were being demolished to make way for the level-crossing in March 1847, with Sandhill House, a property between Lea and Gainsborough being bought to make way for a cutting.

Sensational Diversion

A 'sensation' was caused in Gainsborough, according to the *Lincoln and Stamford Mercury*, by GNR plans to divert a road to make way for the tracks, but a compromise solution was reached after a meeting in the town. The paper later admitted that the anticipated injury to the road was 'more imaginary than real'. In October 1847, the company reached an agreement with the MS&LR that it would make use of the latter's bridge and station there – the current Gainsborough Central.

Work started on Deeping Fen, between Peterborough and Spalding, in September 1847, but was held up at Gainsborough and Lincoln by strikes of bricklayers and labourers. In the first case, the reason was a demand for more money – they were replaced by 'men from Birkenhead', according to one paper, and the second by the failure of a sub-contractor to pay the wages.

At the end of the same month, work finally started in Boston. Peto and Betts, the main contractors, had already opened workshops in the town, and built a wharf in March 1848 to handle imported materials. The bridge itself was completed by June 1848, when a ballast train crossed it heading north. The first few hundred yards, though, included the riverside single track necessitated by the lack of agreement with Councillor Hartley. The final layout was not completed until 1850, after Parliament approved the changes and compensation was paid to Hartley and others.

Work on the timber bridges was held up in June 1848 by a shortage of British oak, needed for Bardney, and again in August when 'a vessel laden with iron' was delayed by stormy weather. Special arrangements had to be made at the Brayford in Lincoln, where the line would cross the navigable Witham on the level. A 'massive iron swing bridge' was to be installed that turned from the centre on a support of iron and oak piles filled with concrete.

Boston as 'the Works'

Boston was a main centre for the GNR, and had hopes of becoming the engineering headquarters of the line. In addition to the passenger and goods facilities, the town also hosted the locomotive department, a gasworks, facilities for creosoting timber sleepers and other woodwork, and a civil engineers' yard. The removal of the locomotive

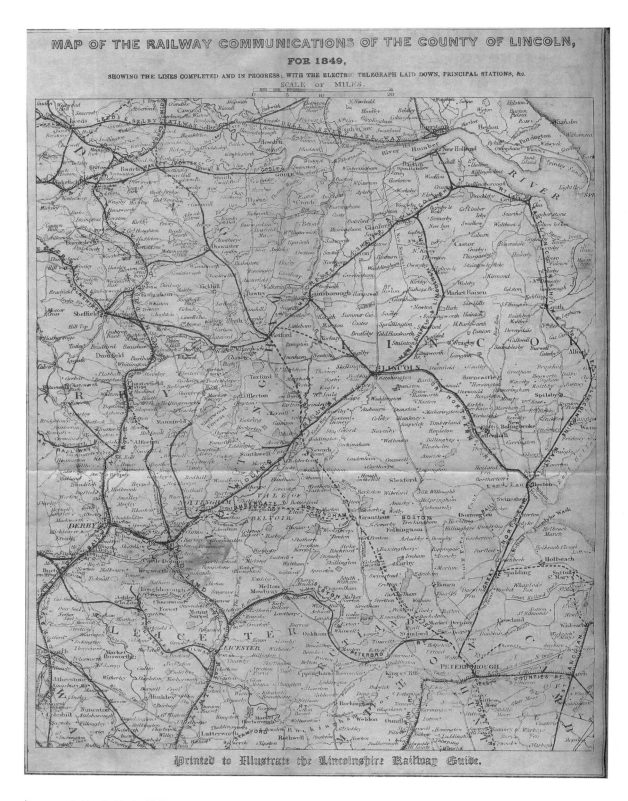

Lines open in Lincolnshire by 1849. ROD KNIGHT

works to Doncaster in 1853 was a blow to the town, since it meant the loss of about 700 jobs in a respected industry.

Between Boston and Lincoln the GNR followed the banks of the River Witham, purchased by the company for that reason, although it meant that trains would be slower on the more winding route. The company did, however, benefit from having to build fewer level-crossings than on most fenland lines, since there were only two bridges over the river between the towns that required access roads, although a number of ferries, also taken over by the railway, did need crossing points.

By the end of August, the line was reported to be complete from Peterborough to Lincoln, other than the bridge at Bardney, and an inspection train traversed the whole distance on 25 September. A train of GNR coaches arrived in Lincoln on 29 September. The *Nottingham Journal* was not impressed by the second-class carriages, which were 'rather circumscribed', to give additional room to the 'particularly elegant' first class.

After inspection by the authorities, the Loop Line from Peterborough to Lincoln was opened on 17 October 1848. Not all the intermediate

stations opened immediately, but by the end of 1849 it was serving Washingborough, Five Mile House, Bardney, Southrey, Stixwould, Kirkstead, Tattershall, Dogdyke and Langrick between Lincoln and Boston; Kirton, Algarkirk and Sutterton and Surfleet from there to Spalding and Littleworth, St James Deeping, and Peakirk on the final stretch to Peterborough. The *Illustrated London News* was not impressed by the GNR's 'plain and inexpensive' architecture, claiming that it killed vernacular styles by avoiding the use of 'more costly kinds of materials and workmanship' in favour of bricks from their own brickworks near Peterborough. Perhaps surprisingly, given the arguments and debates that preceded the opening of the GNR Loop to Lincoln, there are no records of major celebrations in the city. Many locals took the opportunity of a day out in Boston, but even there, the day was only marked by bands, which greeted the midday train from Peterborough. The most exciting moment of the day was probably at about 10.30pm, when the last train from New Holland, running two hours late, crashed through level-crossing gates in Boston; the gate-keeper had gone home some time earlier.

BARDNEY STATION.

'Plain and inexpensive' – Bardney station on the Lincolnshire Loop. ILLUSTRATED LONDON NEWS

Just over a week later, however, on 26 October, Boston celebrated in style, marking what the *Stamford Mercury* described as 'the annihilation of space and time' by the railway. All shops and businesses closed for the day, bells were rung, cannons fired and 2,500 children got the day off school, and free tea and buns. The working classes were treated to a tea and a lecture on the steam engine, and a ball was held so that the ladies should not feel left out.

The main celebration was a 'grand dinner', planned for the Guildhall, but moved to the theatre to provide sufficient space for the 500 guests, including the Earl of Yarborough, two local MPs, officers from all the Lincolnshire railway companies – the GNR and MS&LR had not yet fallen out – a military band and a number of professional singers who entertained the assembled throng. It is likely that everybody there agreed with GNR Chairman, Edmund Denison, that the railway would be 'an imperishable and lasting benefit to Lincolnshire', assuming that they could remember anything that was said due to the effects of the twenty-one toasts taken and responded to.

Flat but Interesting

The *Railway Chronicle*'s correspondent visited the line shortly after it was opened, commenting that the scenery 'though flat, is of a very interesting character'. He was impressed by the speed of construction and the low cost of the lines, putting them down to a combination of the nature of the country and the good sense of the engineer.

> The line is so straight, the country so level, that unless an engineer had gone out of his way to seek reasons for spending money, he could hardly have found the means of erecting any great work. Happily, Mr Cubitt has not gone out of his way for any such purpose.

Over the next few months the Loop was extended north of Lincoln towards Gainsborough, passing through Saxilby, Marton, which later became Stow Park, and Lea on the way. A bridge over the

Fossdyke canal and more challenging countryside than had been met further south slowed the work. Delays were reported in February 1848 due to heavy rain having made work impossible in one of the cuttings and, a month later, by the failure of a bridge.

The line was inspected by Captain Wynne in early April 1849, but the link to the MS&L was not to his satisfaction, so opening was delayed until the ninth. The Trent bridge was not yet open, so the MS&L station at Gainsborough was the terminus of the line for the next few months. The GNR approach was inconvenient, since the trains had to go onto the approach to the bridge, and then reverse back into the station.

No major celebrations were held to mark the opening of this section of the line, although the procession through the town of 400 passengers who had arrived on the Harlequin packet-boat shortly afterwards, on their way by train to a protectionist meeting in Lincoln, would have been a notable sight.

First Trains to New Holland

The MS&LR had meanwhile been making good progress in the north. Work initially concentrated on the section between Grimsby and New Holland,

Spalding station on the Lincolnshire Loop Line of the GNR.
ILLUSTRATED LONDON NEWS

The Great Northern station at Saxilby. The train approaching appears to be headed by MS&L locomotive No 427, built by Neilson in Glasgow and scrapped in 1903.
LINCS TO THE PAST, REF MLL 7979

which opened on 1 March 1848 at the same time as that of 14 miles (22km) of the ELR (now under the control of the GNR) from Grimsby to Louth. There were stations at Goxhill, Ulceby, Habrough, Stallingborough and Great Coates on the MS&LR; and at Ludborough, North Thoresby, Holton-le-Clay and Tetney, and Waltham and Humberstone on the ELR. The New Holland tracks were extended to Barton-upon-Humber in March 1849.

Celebrations of these first sections were relatively subdued, but the *Sheffield and Rotherham Independent* was sufficiently impressed to describe the second-class carriages of the first ELR train as 'comfortably cushioned' with 'very superior workmanship', while the first class had 'rather the

The first train arrives in Grimsby in March 1848. ILLUSTRATED LONDON NEWS

MS&L locomotive and train at Goxhill station. D.N. ROBINSON

The first timetable of the MS&L and ELR. D.N. ROBINSON

appearance of gentlemen's carriages than that of public conveyances'.

Relations between the two companies were amicable at first, with both having running rights over the other's lines, but a deal between the MS&LR and other companies, concerned about the impact on their London traffic of the GNR opening a station there, saw relations cool dramatically. The MS&LR blocked GNR trains from Grimsby station, and therefore from the ferries at New Holland. On one occasion that the GNR did get through, they found the last ferry of the day had been sent off early, so passengers had to spend the night in the train. Through-running on both sets of lines ended in 1851. The GNR did regain access to Grimsby, although its passengers had to change there for New Holland.

The MS&LR line from Ulceby to Brigg by way of Brocklesby and Barnetby opened in September 1848, followed by that from Barnetby to Market Rasen in December 1848 and, later that month, on to Lincoln. There it crossed the GNR line to Boston at Pelham Street and came into the Midland station from the east. The line served Moortown, Holton (later Holton-le-Moor to distinguish it from the ELR station), Usselby, Wickenby, Langworth and Reepham. The opening of the final section between Market Rasen and Lincoln was eagerly anticipated in the former, where 'a grand Dinner and Ball' were planned for the Gordon Arms. 'A pint of wine and dessert' were offered for five shillings (5/- or 25p).

The lines from Grimsby to Lincoln and Brigg did not involve any major engineering works, other than a bridge over the Witham at Lincoln and a deep cutting through Greetwell Hill on the outskirts of the city. The section between Brigg and Gainsborough, with stations at Scawby and Hibaldstow, Kirton Lindsey, Northorpe and Blyton, was a more difficult engineering project. A tunnel through the Lincoln Edge at Kirton required a number of shafts to be dug to allow tunnelling at several different faces. The tunnel was 1,300yd (1,200m) in length and fully lined with brick. When it was completed, the engineer, Mr Fowler, and contractor, Mr Stephenson, 'surveyed it with strictest scrutiny' and declared themselves satisfied. Fowler

1853 photograph of Grimsby Town station. D.N. ROBINSON

paid for a gallon of ale for each of the 130 workmen, while Stephenson contributed 'a first-rate supper' for them all.

Cuttings were required at Kirton, Blyton and Gainsborough, and bridges over the Ancholme and Ancholme Navigation at Brigg and the Trent at Gainsborough. The Ancholme crossings were girder bridges, with embankments required to raise them high enough to give clearance for boats passing underneath.

Gainsborough to Grimsby on a Gala Day

The complete Lincolnshire section of the line from Gainsborough to Grimsby opened in April 1849, and a reporter for the *Stamford Mercury* found that Gainsborough enjoyed 'a gala day ... all the shops were closed and the day was observed as a holiday'. Four directors arrived by train to enjoy 'a superb luncheon' at the White Hart Hotel.

The final element in the MS&LR east–west line was a bridge over the Trent at Bole, just to the south of Gainsborough, described by a newspaper correspondent as 'the greatest engineering feature' of the line east of Sheffield. The Sheffield and Lincolnshire Junction Railway (S&LJR), which had built the line from the west, may well have been happy that the GG&SJ was building the structure, since the S&LJR had suffered major failures of two of its viaducts closer to the city.

The entrance to Kirton tunnel on the MS&L line from Gainsborough to Grimsby. MARK HODSMAN

The bridge had a timber approach from the west 'to afford the least possible obstruction' to the floods that affected the riverside land. Two 'handsome elliptical arches' of stone on each side of the river were linked by two hollow girder bridges resting on the arch abutments and a central pier. The total weight of the ironwork was estimated at just under 400 tons (400,000kg). The original intention was to erect the girders on scaffolding resting on piles in the river, but that proved impractical, and they were eventually built on the eastern approach embankment and winched gradually into place on rollers

The interior of the MS&L/GCR station at Brigg. All the larger stations on the line had overall roofs. D.N. ROBINSON

Class 114 diesel multiple unit (DMU) crossing the Trent Bridge at Gainsborough. JOHN FOREMAN

laid on the piers. Some difficulty was met when the embankments began to settle under the weight of the ironwork, but, after consolidating the structure, the task was completed under the careful eyes of its designer, Mr Fowler, and Mr Fairburn, the manufacturer of the girders.

The successful opening of the bridge in July 1849 allowed trains to run the full distance from Grimsby to Sheffield and beyond, while also giving the GNR access to its own line at Retford. The MS&LR also set out to build their own line – proposed as the Sheffield and Lincolnshire Extension – from Clarborough Junction, just east of Retford, direct to Lincoln by way of Torksey. The plans were changed since the final part into Lincoln paralleled the GNR line to Gainsborough, so the Leverton branch, as it

became known, joined the GNR at Sykes Junction, near Saxilby. The route required another bridge over the Trent, again comprising two tubular girders, each 130ft (40m) in length, resting on stone abutments and a central pier. Fowler was again the engineer concerned, but Board of Trade inspector, Captain Simmonds, was unhappy with the design, despite a test in which six locomotives weighing a total of more than 220 tons only caused a 1in (25mm) movement of the bridge structure. He permitted goods trains to be run over the structure, but Fowler refused to make any changes, and a later inspection cleared the bridge for passenger use in April 1850.

The MS&LR gained running powers into Lincoln over the new line, and the GNR looked for a shorter

The Sheffield and Lincolnshire Extension/MS&L bridge at Torksey.

route to Retford. Sadly, the same dispute that had blocked through-running at Grimsby affected the two companies at Retford, where the MS&LR refused to allow the GNR to use their facilities to take water for its locomotives. However, legal action by the GNR succeeded in gaining access to the water, which they were able to use until their own station opened.

East Lincolnshire Joins Up

Over on the east of the county, the ELR was completing its line between Louth and Boston. The company had not met serious difficulties in the first stage, although the two timber bridges between Louth and Grimsby had to be rebuilt when the foundations gave way in the 'boggy' land. A short masonry viaduct proved more serviceable. On 1 September 1848, 20 miles (32km) of track from Louth to Firsby opened, with stations at Legbourne, Authorpe, Claythorpe, Alford, Willoughby and Burgh-le-Marsh. Again, very little engineering work was involved, apart from the two-arch brick viaduct at Claythorpe and a bridge over the river Lud south of Louth station. What would later be described as a fatal flaw in the construction of the line was the near absence of road bridges. The

forty-nine level-crossings on that stretch alone would prove to be a financial albatross in later years, with similar numbers to be found on all the level stretches.

Six trains ran from Firsby to Grimsby that day, with the first being a seven-carriage parliamentary – one required to be run at a low fare as part of the Enabling Act. Like most such trains, it ran at the least convenient times.

The final 14 miles (22km) into the temporary GNR station in Boston opened a month later on 2 October. The line was dead straight from Burgh to the curve into Boston, passing through Little Steeping, East Ville and New Leake, and Hobhole, named after the adjacent drain. Perhaps sadly, Hobhole was soon changed to the more prosaic – to Lincolnshire ears at least – Leake and Wrangle, then Old Leake and Wrangle, and finally Old Leake, all in the space of three years. There were seven viaducts, no road bridges and a further forty-six level-crossings. One 90ft (27m) iron bridge crossed the Maud Foster Drain close to Boston, and the tracks cross the Hobhole Drain at such an acute angle that the waterway appears to tunnel under the line.

Two weeks after the full opening, the *Doncaster, Nottingham and Lincoln Gazette* reported that the

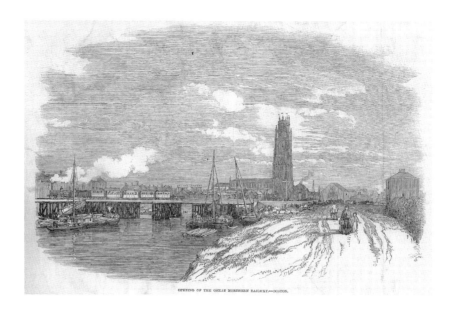

Boston at the opening of the Lincolnshire Loop and ELR in 1848.
ILLUSTRATED LONDON NEWS

The substantial Firsby station on the East Lincolnshire Railway. D.N. ROBINSON

company had taken just over £61,000 in receipts since the initial partial opening, with expenses about half that figure. The *Railway Chronicle* was most impressed by these early financial returns:

> The shareholders of the Great Northern are to be congratulated on the wise management of their affairs, so as to give them at so early a period and so small a cost a beneficial return on the money already spent. By it, a large district, largely cut off from the benefits of railway communication, is now opened up and one of the producing and agricultural districts of England is brought into connexion with the metropolis, and with the consuming districts which will henceforth be the most profitable market for its produce.

Great Northern Links to London and York

Meantime, the GNR had been busy both to the north and south of Lincolnshire. Into Yorkshire it was laying track from Retford to Doncaster, ready to carry the trains due to arrive by way of the MS&LR from the Loop. The lawyers were also busy, since the company wanted to change the route north of Gainsborough from one that would have joined the Towns Line at Bawtry to a more direct route towards Doncaster. The proposed change was not approved by Parliament, partly due to the objections of people like the hunting gentleman referred to earlier, so the MS&LR connection at Retford remained in use.

To the south, the GNR main line to King's Cross was being constructed by Thomas Brassey, while, between Peterborough and Retford, work was going on in preparation for the GNR's Towns Line, including the important Lincolnshire section around Grantham; but there will be more on that in the next chapter.

The Ambergate Arrives – and Stops

One other important rail link entered the county in 1850, although only just. On 15 July, the Ambergate, Nottingham and Boston and Eastern Junction Railway opened for business at the Canal Wharf in Grantham, having made its way there from Nottingham. Goods traffic started a week later, but the intention to continue the line to Sleaford and Boston was not carried through. The company ran out of money, although, according to railway engineer, David Joy, it did amaze the country population:

One of the funs of the place was its being a new line, everybody and everything was strange to the engines. People used to come and get on to the line at the road crossing gates and wave their umbrellas at us to stop as if we were an old stage-coach: We didn't. Then the game, and cows and sheep used to stare. We picked up lots of game, especially at night, when they ran at the lights.

The Ambergate may have been stuck on a wharf side in Grantham, but with the completion of the GNR loop, the ELR and the MS&LR main line, the basic structure of Lincolnshire's railways was in place. There were still plenty of gaps to be filled and dreams to be demolished: the Towns Line was incomplete; the question of the link with the eastern counties had not yet been sorted; and Boston was still without its link to the Midlands; but Lincolnshire was well and truly on the railway map.

CHAPTER 4

Filling the Gaps

All Change in Lincolnshire

The arrival of railways in Lincolnshire set off a large number of changes in the county; some were beneficial, others less so. On the good side, communications speeded up significantly. A trip to London from Lincoln by stagecoach took eighteen hours in the 1840s, but this fell to less than seven when the Midland offered connections by way of Nottingham in 1846, with a further two-and-a-half-hour reduction in 1850 when through trains were available by way of the GNR through Peterborough. The royal family used the Loop Line and the MS&LR in 1851 on their way to Scotland, although it is reported that Queen Victoria refused to get out of the train in Lincoln to meet local dignitaries. Apparently the MP for Lincoln had voted against an increased allowance for her husband, Prince Albert, and she had decided not to set foot in the town while he was still in office. Albert himself had passed through the city earlier, in 1849, on his way to lay the foundation stone for the new docks at Grimsby being developed by the railways.

The *Railway Chronicle* of 21 October 1848 was particularly impressed by the way that the GNR was able to offer much faster and cheaper passenger and goods services between Hull and London:

A traveller can now be carried in a first-class train for 32/- [£1.60]; 1 cwt of fish can be taken from Hull to London in eight to ten hours for 2/6d [12.5p] or a parcel of 56lb can be carried at less than a penny a pound for the whole distance. These are fares that must invite traffic and which the smallness of the capital expended can alone justify.

Locally, a trip from Lincoln to Boston took less than an hour-and-a-half, compared to several times that period by river-packet, although the boats did manage to stay in business for a number of years

Fen celery, a traffic that benefited by faster transport to regional and national markets. STUART GIBBARD

GNR excursion notice 1870. ROD KNIGHT

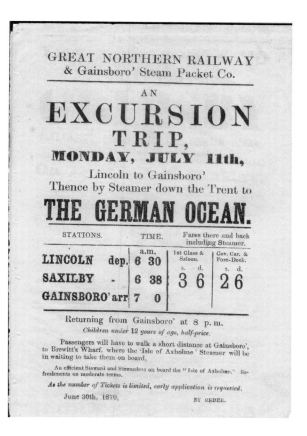

despite what might be described as 'loss-leader' pricing tactics by the railway. Some people just preferred the boat trip. Short journeys were more important than had been expected. The *Railway Times* noted with apparent surprise that first-class passengers only travelled 26 miles (42km) on average, while second and third covered 13 and 11 miles (21 and 18km), respectively:

> It is clear that the railways derive their revenue from passengers who travel short distances, and not from those who pass between the great centres of population which mark its termini.

Excursions by train became popular. The GNR completed its link to Doncaster just in time to run trips to the races there in 1849; the temperance movement and religious revivals drew large crowds to their meetings; fairs, shows and events such as the Great Exhibition of 1851 were easier

Coal being bagged up for onward delivery by Borman & Son at Skegness station in 1910. STEVE PRIESTLEY

to attend; and people began discovering the health benefits of sea air – a development that was to play a major part in the history of Lincolnshire's railways. Such trips might only cost a few pence, but served to broaden the horizons of the local population, much as had been feared by Col. Sibthorp and his friends!

Goods coming into the county also came down dramatically in price. Coal, the principal commodity carried by the early railways, fell from 40–50 shillings (£2–£2.50) a ton when delivered by sea and road to less than 30 shillings (£1.50) in the countryside and just over a pound in Lincoln and other larger towns. The coal merchant became a regular station feature, with coal delivered by wagon, unloaded by hand and bagged up, again by hand, for sale to local customers.

Manure and lime to improve farmland, and bricks, tiles and timber for building fell in price or became available at places previously unable to obtain them. Agricultural produce was the main outgoing trade, with grain, pulses, wool and even reeds for thatching carried regularly. Other local crops, such as flowers and potatoes, increased in importance once quick and easy transport became available and markets developed. Livestock no longer needed to be driven tens of miles to markets, but could be loaded onto trains for distant locations.

One report from the 1854 Spring Fair at Market Rasen expressed amazement at how '100 beasts [sold there] were dispatched by rail and would reach Norwich the same evening'.

Communications also improved for those who did not want to travel. The invention of the Penny Post and the ability of the railways to carry it saw the number of letters delivered rise from 76 million in 1838 to over 640 million in 1864.

Engineering Benefits

The railways also encouraged the development of major agricultural engineering companies in the county. Marshall's of Gainsborough had sidings directly into the MS&LR station in the town; Clayton and Shuttleworth in Lincoln, although established shortly before the railways, found new markets, and were soon joined by Ruston's and Robey's; while Grantham and its railways provided an excellent base for Richard Hornsby. Ironically, the best-established engineering firm in the county in the 1830s and 1840s, Tuxford's of Boston, failed to thrive in the railway era, possibly partly due to their lack of convenient connections with the lines.

The county's ports experienced very different effects. Gainsborough and Boston saw initial increases in traffic as materials for the new rail-

Maltings at Grimsby took in barley from farms in the area and converted it into malt for brewing beer or spirits.
D.N. ROBINSON

AGRICULTURAL MEETING AT LINCOLN: MESSRS. CLAYTON AND SHUTTLEWORTH'S WORKS, AND THE SHOW YARD.—SEE PAGE 175.

Drawing of Clayton and Shuttleworth works in Lincoln showing railway and waterway links.

ways were brought in during the construction phase, but then fell back to well below previous levels. The prospectus for the Wakefield Lincoln and Boston Railway (WL&BR) had predicted that large amounts of coal would be transported by rail from Yorkshire then by boat from Boston, but the reality was that the GNR, which had taken over the proposed routes and rights granted to the WL&BR by its parliamentary bill, kept the coal for themselves and moved it by rail direct to London. The port lost a third of its coal trade between 1848 and 1854 rather than the expected increase.

Grimsby, by contrast, blossomed under the care of the MS&LR. The Dock Company itself was a major backer of the company, which returned the favour many times over. For example, 138 acres of land were reclaimed and 20 acres of new docks created. Lock gates and other machinery were operated by hydraulic power – the first major harbour to be so equipped – with the entire system driven by the pressure generated by the distinctive 300ft (100m) Dock Tower. The railway company then enticed a number of fishermen to base themselves at Grimsby; founded, with the GNR and Midland Railway (MR), the Deep Sea Fishing Company; and built a separate 6-acre fish dock and floating pontoon to encourage the new activity. Grimsby had real cause to be grateful for the presence of the railways, and would continue to be so for many years to come.

Catching Up With the Early Birds

The benefits of the railways having become clear to those communities served by them, many other parts of the county were now keen to catch up, but there was also a significant gap still to be closed. Peterborough had to be linked to Retford, to complete the Towns Line from London to the north. The most difficult section was that from Corby Glen, just south of Grantham, through the town to Hougham, a few miles north. It included two tunnels – Stoke and Peascliff – and a number of significant earthworks. Thomas Jackson, of Pimlico, was awarded the contract in September 1849 after a delay caused by discussions as to whether the line should make use of the existing Barrowby tunnel dug by the Ambergate, rather than the planned one at Peascliff. The 'Barrowby Deviation' was surveyed by Joseph Cubitt, the GNR's engineer, but he decided against it, and Jackson began work laying out the route in December 1849, with digging under way by March of the following year. The *Nottingham Journal* reported that 150 men were 'staking out, levelling and sawing timber' and the *Lincoln and Stamford Mercury* informed its readers that 'the cutting through Spitalgate Hill … is in active process'.

Jackson and his men faced a massive task. In addition to the tunnels, they were required to dig the cuttings on the approaches to them, which required the removal of about 1½ million cubic yards (1.15 million cubic metres) of earth. Contracts were let on the basis that a labourer could remove 10–12cu. yd ($7–9m^3$) a day, so the tunnels alone represented something on the order of 150,000 man-days of effort. A tax on bricks, imposed to help pay for the wars against the American colonies, was repealed in 1850, which delayed tunnel-lining because the builders waited for the price to fall before buying their bricks. There were then further delays as the pent-up demand resulted in a national brick shortage and another while Jackson and the company argued about whether the reduced cost should be reflected in his payment.

Work on the tunnel linings finally began in earnest in October 1850, although Jackson admitted that he only had enough bricks for about a fifth of the final length. It had been hoped that the work would be completed by September 1851, but delays were accumulating, and discussions took place with the various contractors to see if work could be accelerated by additional payments. No agreement is recorded, and the company's agent commented that he had not been surprised since 'each is willing to take his own risk, but will not trust the others'.

The weather during the winter of 1850–51 slowed work other than in the tunnels, with heavy rain in March making progress on the earthworks hard to achieve. Rain again delayed work in June and in August, with the chance to make up time in July lost by the number of men who left their jobs to work on farms getting in the hay. A further six weeks were lost later in the summer by the 'total stagnation' during the grain harvest, but Jackson gave his 'distinct and positive personal assurance' that more men would be employed to catch up. Spitalgate cutting, in particular, became notorious as a source of trouble and discontent: 'It is full of springs and is described as being in motion since the face was cut away'.

Further south, between Peterborough and Jackson's area round Grantham, a tender for the work by Messrs Warren and Delroche was initially accepted, subject to good references from the Great Western's Isambard Kingdom Brunel. Such references may not have been forthcoming, since the contract was changed to Messrs Pearce and Smith in May of 1850. Delays in obtaining possession of the land required meant that work did not start until October, followed within a month by requests from the contractors for more money to ensure completion by September 1851. Lack of bricks again caused delays, in this case for the construction of bridges and flood-control works, and rain again slowed work on cuttings and embankments. Mention of the 1851 target disappears from the reports, and the contractors are praised for their efforts, completing the job by February 1852 thanks to 'fair exertion and good management'.

Grantham Great Northern station.

D.N. ROBINSON

One Out, All Out

Things were proving less straightforward on the Grantham section. The strike referred to in the previous chapter hit Jackson and his subcontractors in December 1851. A dispute with a ganger about the workload escalated when, according to the *Lincolnshire Chronicle*, their employer told them 'they would be glad to eat hay and straw before the winter was over' if they didn't go back to work. The arguments had started in the Spitalgate cutting, but the men soon got the backing of their colleagues in most of the other working locations. A meeting in a Grantham pub failed to settle the matter, but a troop of soldiers from Nottingham backed the police and magistrates in arresting what were seen as the ringleaders. They were sent to the local jail in Folkingham and the men returned to work. As mentioned earlier, the soldiers then got drunk and had to be sent back to Nottingham, while the *Lincolnshire Chronicle* came out in support of the men about whom 'ridiculous accounts' had been circulating:

> One paper stated that the navvies were going about Grantham intimidating their employers, the authorities and the inhabitants, and threatening to blow up the town ... [but] no outrage was committed on the town and the only illegal act was trespassing on the works and driving off such men as were inclined to work.

More engineering problems were met. A three-arch bridge over the Witham sank into soft ground and had to be rebuilt; the Spitalgate cutting continued to subside, bringing down with it the bridge that carried the Great North Road over the line and the town water supply, resulting in Grantham being without mains water for two days. The southernmost clay cutting of their contract got so wet and unworkable that Pearce and Smith had to be brought in to ballast and lay track for 3 miles (5km) to the north of their completed section.

Money was a continuing problem. The line should have opened on 15 June 1852, but Jackson was still arguing about the brick tax rebate, among other things, and had delayed completion of the work. Joseph Cubitt described him as 'languid and unsatisfactory' and, later that month, ended his contract and took control of the works himself. The *Lincoln and Stamford Mercury* wrote of him standing on the line, determined 'to put an end to the child's play going on and finish the works regardless of Mr Jackson's contract'.

The works were finally completed by early July, inspected on the 12th and 13th and opened for business on the 15th. The section beyond Grantham through Nottinghamshire to Retford had already been completed, so the Towns Line was now able to go into full operation, with the fast services transferred from the Loop to the new route. Celebrations in Grantham were, according to the *Lincoln, Rutland and Stamford Mercury*, 'one of the quietest affairs of which, in reference to so vast an under-

taking, it is possible to conceive'. Major events had been planned for the June date, but had been cancelled, no doubt to the great regret of the thousand men who were to 'receive beef and ale' or the like number of women who were to be offered tea. Mr Jackson, it was noted, had declined to contribute to the celebrations.

Even with the line open, the company's troubles were not over. A large slippage in the Spitalgate cutting derailed a train on 13 October, while another a few days later trapped a man who was working in a shaft being used to drain water from the area.

Nottingham Blocked

The Ambergate moved its passenger terminus into the GNR station on 1 August 1852, although sidings at the old Wharf station remained in service for goods until the 1980s. The GNR thought it had scored a victory when it gained control of the Ambergate, which it believed gave it the smaller company's rights to run into Nottingham. Unfortunately, the Ambergate only had access to that city by way of running powers over two Midland branches and the Midland, which had tried to take it over themselves, did not take kindly to the arrival of the GNR. They gained an injunction to prevent the GNR from operating the Ambergate, who then ran a train under their own name, but with a loco hired from the GNR. In scenes reminiscent of the earlier disputes with the MS&LR, on arrival at Nottingham the loco was 'hustled away by a number of Midland engines, trapped in a shed and the access rails lifted'. The courts agreed that the Midland had the right to do that, and a wider agreement was reached between the MR and the GNR about sharing the receipts for all the traffic travelling between a number of towns that were served by both companies.

Branching Out

Within the county, several well-established market towns were beginning to feel the lack of railway connections. Horncastle, Spilsby, Caistor, Sleaford and others had all featured on earlier plans, but had not been connected. The GNR and the MS&LR both had additional powers or projects in hand, but had found the experience of building their original lines more costly than expected and saw cooperation with local promoters as a better way forward in many cases.

Horncastle and its Horses

The first town to promote its own line was Horncastle, in the centre of the county, which backed the Horncastle and Kirkstead Junction Railway to link the town with the Lincolnshire Loop at Kirkstead. The prospectus spoke of the general benefits to trade, but made specific warning of the risk to the business of the town, particularly its large annual horse fair, if no line was built:

> Unless the Owners of property, and all parties interested in the prosperity of the Town and its Neighbourhood, unite to assist in carrying out the present Railway, the business of Horncastle Horse Fair (as well as the Corn and Cattle Markets), will gradually diminish, while the Fairs and Markets of other towns possessing Railway accommodation are increasing.

It was a very local affair: only three members of the committee of forty-four were not from within 5 miles (8km) of the town, with the large majority farmers or local traders. The Act was obtained on 10 July 1854, and celebrated when the news arrived at 10pm, by 'a joyous peal of the parish church bells being rung, and crowds parading the streets'. A flag, bearing the words 'God speed the railway' was flown from the church the following day and crowds, led by the town band, again passed through the streets.

Construction began in April the following year on a very straightforward basis. The line was only 7 miles (11km) long, had a single over-bridge and one station between the two end-points, at the recently established health resort at Woodhall Spa; it opened on 17 August. Rather in contrast to the Grantham situation, the inhabitants of Horncastle, who had planned the opening celebration for the 11 August, stuck to that date and celebrated the event six days before an official train ran.

The original capital of the Horncastle company was £48,000, in £10 shares, and the final cost at about £60,000 was met by taking out additional loans. The GNR ran the line from the beginning,

Prospectus of the Horncastle and Kirkstead Junction Railway.

paying half the receipts to the shareholders; and the enterprise proved profitable. Rev. Walter noted with some satisfaction, that the £10 shares were worth nearly £15 in 1907. It never failed to pay a dividend up to the point it lost its independence in 1923.

Boston Gets its Western Gateway

Boston's initial enthusiasm for railways had waned somewhat in the early 1850s, as the GNR took away the coastal coal trade that it had hoped to gain from the Wakefield link, and the Ambergate remained stalled at Grantham.

The situation began to improve in 1853, when the Boston, Sleaford and Midland Counties Railway (BS&MCR) was authorized to complete what the

A GRAND CEREMONY FOR HORNCASTLE

A full description of the opening of the Horncastle and Kirkstead Junction Railway is to be found in James Conway Walter's *A History of Horncastle from the Earliest Period to the Present Time*:

At an early hour the town was crowded with visitors and shops were closed. At 7 a.m. 2,500 lbs. of beef were distributed among the poorer people. Peals of bells were rung; the Horncastle and Spilsby bands added their music of popular airs. The streets and station were profusely decorated, under the direction of Mr. Crowder, florist, Mr. John Osborne, parish clerk, Mr. Archbould, head gardener to Sir H. Dymoke, Mr. Nelson from Stourton Hall, and a local committee. Flags displayed the arms of the town, those of Sir H. Dymoke, Mr. J. Banks Stanhope, the Bishop of Carlisle, then lord of the manor, the Rose of England, and the Union Jack. About noon a procession was formed in the Bull Ring, to meet the Directors of the G.N.R., by Mr. F. Harwood, master of the ceremonies, in the following order:

Navvy bearing bronzed pickaxe and shovel.
Banner.
Navvies, four abreast.
Banner.
Two navvies, bearing silver-gilt wheelbarrow.
Banners.
Horncastle Brass Band.
Contractor. Engineer.
Secretary. Solicitor.
Auditor. Auditor.
Banners. Directors, two abreast. Banners.
Churchwarden, Dr. B. J. Boulton.
The Vicar, Rev. W. H. Milner.
Banners. Shareholders and their friends, four Banners.
abreast.
Spilsby Brass Band.
Parish Clerk, Mr. J. C. Osborne, in his
robes, preceded by his Standard Bearer.
Banner. Members of the various Clubs, with Banner.
Banners.
Banner. 1,000 School Children, 4 abreast. Banner.
The Public.

The procession marched from the Bull Ring to the Railway Station, where the elders of the party on the platform, and the children, with their banners, ranged on the opposite side, awaited the arrival of the train bringing the G.N.R. Directors, and as it drew up the bands played 'See the Conquering Hero comes'.

The procession, augmented by the directors, then reformed, and marched through the town; in the Bull Ring the National Anthem was sung. A large marquee was erected, in which the contractors, Messrs. Smith & Knight, provided for the directors and shareholders, and other guests, in all over 200, a splendid dinner, served in excellent style. The Honble. Sir H. Dymoke presided, as Chairman of the Horncastle and Kirkstead Railway Co.; being supported on his right by Mr. Hussey Packe and Mr. C. Chaplin, Directors of the G.N.R., Major Amcotts and Sir M. J. Cholmeley, and on his left by J. Banks Stanhope, Esq., M.P., Director of the Horncastle Railway, and Rev. W. H. Milner, Vicar. Congratulatory speeches were made, and the day closed with a fine display of fireworks.

Not everybody was convinced that the line would be a success!

Ambergate had set out to do. The company was solidly backed by the GNR, and ran from their Towns Line at Barkston, just north of Grantham, then by way of Sleaford to a junction with the Loop Line at Boston. This was a more northerly route than that proposed by the Ambergate, which would have run south of Sleaford, passing through the old market and coaching town of Folkingham.

The BS&MCR took advantage of the Ancaster Gap in the Heath to minimize gradients and engineering work between Barkston and Sleaford. A cutting and climb was required at Wilsford, just east of Ancaster, although the drawing in the *Illustrated London News* perhaps overemphasized the obstacles concerned. The 11-mile (18km) section to Sleaford was built by Smith, Knight & Co. and was

Hanbeck Quarry cutting near Wilsford on the Boston, Sleaford and Midland Counties. ILLUSTRATED LONDON NEWS

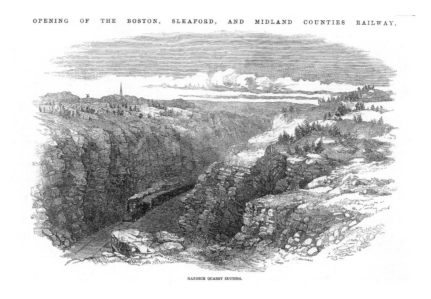

OPENING OF THE BOSTON, SLEAFORD, AND MIDLAND COUNTIES RAILWAY.

HANBECK QUARRY CUTTING.

formally opened on Tuesday 16 June 1857, with stations at Honington and Ancaster, although records exist for celebrations the previous Saturday – the 13th. These involved the closure of all businesses in Sleaford, a procession and a dinner in tents on the cricket field for 'all the working men' from the immediate vicinity. The tents, though, had to be 'vacated at or before 5 o'clock to allow of provision being made for the General Tea Drinking'. Tea and cake were provided 'for the women' and all the scholars of the town received 'a silver Three-pence and a bun'.

Sleaford station in Great Northern days. D.N. ROBINSON

THE STATION HECKINGTON.

Heckington station at some point after 1892, the date that the eight-sailed cap was fitted to the windmill.
ROD KNIGHT

The final 17-mile (27km) section of the line from Sleaford to Boston ran almost due east across the Fens to Boston, with stations at Heckington and Swineshead. In what was by now almost a tradition of the GNR in the Fens, it ran for part of its way on the banks of a waterway, in this case the South Forty-Foot Drain. As was usually the case in the area, engineering was uncomplicated, consisting mainly of bridges over watercourses. Services began on Tuesday 12 April 1859 with an additional station at Hubbard's Bridge, later changed to Hubbert's Bridge, added in May 1860. The trains proved popular with travellers from the intermediate stations – sometimes too popular. On 16 May 1859 so many people turned up at Heckington for the train to Sleaford that a hundred had to be left behind. The station master refused to refund their fares resulting in 'a scene of disorder and dissatisfaction' according to the Sleaford paper. On the western section, a station at Barkston, to permit easier exchange of passengers to and from the north, was brought into use on 1 July 1867. When built, the line was single-tracked, but was doubled in the later 1870s. The BS&MC was another of the lines taken over by the GNR on 1 January 1865.

Spilsby and Sheep

The market town of Spilsby, on the eastern side of the Wolds, noted the success of its neighbour, Horncastle, in building and running a successful small railway, and, worried about the loss of its trade to neighbouring towns, decided to follow suit. A meeting was held in the town on 31 October 1864 and the arguments proved so persuasive that enough shares in the Spilsby and Firsby Railway (S&FR) were sold at the meeting, and immediately afterwards, that the surveyors were at work within a week!

An agreement was quickly reached with the East Lincolnshire that the 4-mile (7km) line would join its tracks at Firsby, and the GNR agreed in April 1865 to operate the line for twenty-one years in return for 40 per cent of the receipts. The company was authorized on 5 July of the same year.

Unfortunately, such swift progress was not to continue. Share sales fell back, and construction did not begin until 14 May 1867, accompanied by the kind of celebrations usually only seen on the arrival of the first trains. Shops were closed, bunting and flags hung out and a procession wound through the

Sheep could be a valuable trade. The crate about to be loaded into this wagon at Kirkstead station is marked 'Buenos Aires'. Lincoln Longwool rams were sold to Argentina for up to 1,000 guineas – £1,050 – at the turn of the nineteenth century.

town to the site of the station. The first sod was cut by the Rev. Edward Rawnsley, who had chaired that first meeting nearly three years earlier. He was followed to the ceremonial silver spade by three local dignitaries, six wives and a small boy. It is reported that each lady performed her 'somewhat novel task with considerable tact' and was greeted with loud applause.

The line was built by Messrs Barnes and Beckett for just over £23,000 paid roughly half and half in cash and shares. Contractors holding shares had proved to cause difficulties on other lines in the past, and the company bought them back and sold them to other shareholders. Despite the fact that £10 shares were sold for less than a third of that price, it was estimated to have saved the company several thousand pounds in reduced commitments to the contractors.

The single-track line reached Firsby in August 1867, and was inspected by the government

Spilsby GNR station. GREAT NORTHERN RAILWAY SOCIETY

inspector Captain Tyler and officials of the GNR during the winter. Following a number of improvements, services began on 1 May 1868.

Sadly, the line never lived up to the hopes of its founders. Passenger traffic was steady but unexciting and goods were the usual mix of coal, fertilizer and other agricultural requirements and general merchandise. Spilsby did have the equivalent of the Horncastle Horse Fair in the Partney Sheep Fairs, held about 2 miles (3km) away, where thousands of sheep were traded, particularly at the Partney Great Fair, held in the autumn. Many of those animals would have passed through the station, and there are reports of the confusion that could ensue while trying to sort and load them, thirty at a time, into cattle trucks. The profitability of such business was affected by the need to send extra railway staff to Spilsby to help with the loading and paperwork. A horse and a handler were provided to pull filled and empty wagons to and from the loading bays, work that would have been inconvenient and expensive to carry out with a locomotive.

A single intermediate station serving the village of Halton Holegate never generated much in the way of revenue and the S&FR struggled financially throughout its existence. No dividends were paid on the shares for the first decade of its existence, and,

although shareholders did get a return from then till 1885, it never went above 4 per cent. The GNR took the company over in 1889 for £20,000 and ran it from 1 January 1891.

The situation might have improved if either of the plans to link the Horncastle and Spilsby branches had been carried out, giving the GNR a more direct link from Lincoln to the coast, but the final scheme, the Lincoln, Horncastle, Spilsby and East Coast Railway faded away in the late 1880s.

Given the experience of our final line for this chapter, it was probably just as well that the link was not attempted. Punching through the Lincolnshire Wolds was to prove to be a more difficult task than expected.

Struggling Over the Wolds

The Louth and Lincoln Railway (L&LR) was launched with a great burst of enthusiasm and some wildly optimistic predictions of trade. Proposed at a meeting in Louth on 3 November 1865, the line would run from the East Lincolnshire, just south of Louth station, to a junction with the Lincolnshire Loop at Five Mile House. It was expected to attract much of the passenger and goods trade between the two conurbations away from the

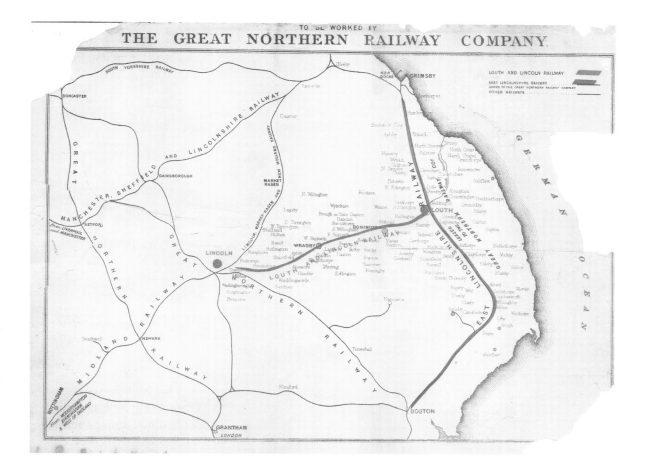

Map from the prospectus of the Louth and Lincoln Railway.

existing circuitous routes by way of Grimsby or Boston, as well as carrying manufactured goods from the Midlands to Grimsby, and passengers to Cleethorpes, 'the Margate of the Midlands', according to the prospectus.

Such claims were fairly standard for railway promoters of the day, but where the Louth and Lincoln really went over the top was in their predictions of the mineral traffic that would originate from the vicinity of the line or which would be carried from the East Midlands coalfields.

The prospectus calculated that the line would carry 300,000 tons of coal – most of it for export,

since the local market was only estimated to be 50,000 tons/year – and a quarter of a million tons of ironstone. Engineer Thomas Myers, in a letter that accompanied the prospectus, suggested that 'the District ... holds out considerable advantages for the manufacture of iron of very superior quality', which could be shipped to the Continent and all over Britain in a condition 'to compete with any Pig Iron ... in England'.

Some ironstone is to be found in the Wolds, and has been mined in later years, but the quantities were never sufficient to have provided the L&LR with the predicted traffic.

South Willingham signal box. GN train approaching from Louth. D.N. ROBINSON

The company got its bill approved in August 1866, but lack of money caused the directors to apply to Parliament in 1870 for permission to abandon the project. Permission was refused, and the company struggled on by handing the whole project to Mr Frederick Appleby, a civil engineer from Manchester. Appleby shortened the line and reduced the worst of the gradients by adding two tunnels at Withcall and South Willingham. It had also not been possible to acquire the land needed at Five Mile House to build the junction, so a new connection was proposed at Bardney. This had to join the Loop in the Boston direction, which meant that trains could not run through to Lincoln without reversing.

Construction began in July 1872, but bad weather slowed construction, and the company took control again. Conditions in the tunnels led to a strike of bricklayers and the GNR insisted on cash up front for putting in the connections at Louth and Bardney. The line eventually opened in stages. That from Bardney to South Willingham carried goods from 9 November 1874, followed by an extension to Donington on Bain on 27 September the following year. By 26 June 1876, goods traffic was using the whole distance, but passengers had to wait a further six months following problems detected by the Board of Trade inspector.

The line served seven stations, at Kingthorpe, Wragby, East Barkwith, Hainton and South Willingham, Donington on Bain, Withcall and Hallington, of which only Wragby offered any real chance of profitable traffic. The line struggled financially from the outset and went into receivership in 1881. The GNR bought it later that year for about half of what it had cost to build.

The Great Northern and its allies and subsidiaries now had effective control of most of the railways of central Lincolnshire. The situation in the north and south of the county was more complicated.

CHAPTER 5

The Eastern Comeback

Although the attempt to make the eastern approach to Lincolnshire into the main line to the north had failed, the south of the county still saw a great deal of railway activity over the second half of the nineteenth century. Most of it consisted of renewed attempts to create lines to the north or across the southern Fens, but there was a rush of activity in the south-west corner of the county.

The Marquis of Exeter's Railway

The Stamford and Essendine Railway was Stamford's response to being missed by the Great Northern's main line. Whether that lack of connection was because, as is widely held, the Marquis of Exeter refused to allow the line to cross part of his Burghley Park estate, or whether it was simply a matter of engineering convenience, is unlikely to be settled after this length of time. The fact remains that Stamford felt that it needed a shorter connection to this new line, despite it already having a link with it at Peterborough, and the strong support provided by the Marquis, who was the majority shareholder, helped ensure that link.

The line was only a little over 3 miles (5km) long with just one station, Ryhall and Belmesthorpe, between Stamford and the junction with the GNR at Essendine. There were no major earthworks or tunnelling, which makes it all the more surprising

The train shed at Stamford East station 0–6–0 no. 195 waits to leave on a train to Essendine and no. 161, a 0–4–2 saddle tank built in 1877, heads a train for Wansford. D.N. ROBINSON

that a line that got its Act in 1853 did not open until November 1856. It was built for £46,000 by Thomas Hayton, who died before it was finished, which may explain part of the delay.

From 1864 to 1872 the GNR stopped working the Stamford-to-Essendine Line, and the Marquis of Exeter assumed responsibility. His coat of arms was painted on the doors of the first-class carriages and it is probably from this period that the alternative title of 'the Marquis of Exeter's Railway' originates. His influence was also felt in the construction of the

Stamford.   The G. N. R. Station and Welland River.

The Stamford and Essendine/GNR station at Stamford.

stone-built Stamford station, known as Stamford East to differentiate it from the Midland's Stamford Town. It echoed the grand Tudor style of Burghley House, and the Marquis's arms are incorporated into the gables of the station.

Despite the fact that the railway never made much money, in February 1867 it invested in an 8-mile (13km) branch from Stamford to Wansford, on the Northampton-to-Peterborough Line of the London and North Western, with stations at Barnack, Ufford, Wansford Road and Wansford. Known locally as 'the Bread-and-Onion Line', the intention was to get a faster connection through to London, but the line faded out through lack of traffic. In 1872 the GNR took both lines back under its wing.

Lord Willoughby's Railway

The Marquis of Exeter and Lord Brownlow were both initially unhappy about the coming of the railways, but Lincolnshire's aristocracy in general were more supportive. One of the most enthusiastic was Peter Robert, 21st Baron Willoughby de Eresby and 2nd Baron Gwydyr, usually known as Lord Willoughby, who built his own line across his estates at Grimsthorpe Castle, near Bourne. The 4 miles (7km) of track ran from the GNR Towns Line station at Little Bytham to the village of Edenham, a mile from the castle itself. Lord Willoughby was a keen supporter of agricultural innovation, and

had originally built a road link to Little Bytham, with a traction engine to haul incoming coal and outgoing produce. The engine, *Ophir*, was designed by the Great Western's Daniel Gooch, but could not manage the bends and gradients on the road. Experiments were carried out on a tramway but in early 1855, his Lordship decided to build it as a railway. *Ophir* was converted to run on tracks, gradients were eased and rails were laid, Great Western fashion, using short, longitudinal timber sleepers. The line came into use that November.

As a private railway, the Edenham Branch, sometimes called 'the Edenham and Little Bytham Railway', did not need parliamentary approval, but it did need to be inspected before it could carry passengers. A survey by Lt. Col. Yolland in 1856 showed that the line was nowhere near the standards required. There were no signals, poor drainage, the wrong kind of ballast, insecure rail joints, outdated pointwork and, most important, the lack of transverse sleepers meant that the track gauge could not be maintained correctly. George Scott, the Grimsthorpe estate bailiff, who oversaw much of the work on the railway, noted, with apparent surprise, the 'astonishing difference' in the running of the engine on the parts of the line where transverse sleepers were installed.

Havilah, Lord Willoughby's second engine. BRIAN LAWRENCE

Two more inspections were unsatisfactory but, on 22 July 1857, Yolland finally allowed passengers to be carried, albeit with severe speed restrictions of 15mph (24km/h) overall but 8mph (13km/h) on curves and a maximum weight for a locomotive of 12 tons (12,000kg). An earlier accident involving *Havilah*, the company's second locomotive, and the continuing lack of signals, resulted in only one engine allowed in steam at any time. It had been hoped that the GNR would take over the operation following approval, but they declined the offer, so Lord Willoughby himself took on the responsibility. Passenger service began on 8 December 1857 using coaches hired in from the GNR, who also rented the company a second-hand locomotive. The line struggled to cover costs, and Scott, now railway manager as well as bailiff, had difficulties with Lord Willoughby's son, Alberic Drummond. Drummond expected a train to be sent for him if he arrived late at Little Bytham, and persuaded a driver to cut the usual journey time to that station from the official twenty minutes to a mere nine, in order to catch a main-line service.

Rise and Fall

In 1858, a third engine, *Columbia*, was added to the stud, and the railway ordered two coaches to their own design from the GNR works at Doncaster. For two years the company did well, although it relied on coal for over 80 per cent of its income. That trade was lost in 1860 when the GNR branch from Essendine to Bourne opened, with the coal business subsidized by them. The Edenham branch tried to compete by improving its services and track but the writing was on the wall. Various takeovers were proposed, but none carried through. The death of Lord Willoughby in 1865 was probably the last straw for the line, although his funeral, in March, did result in a number of additional trains being run, including a special from Firsby, carrying tenants and staff from estate lands in the north of the county.

The railway struggled on for a few more years, but the residual passenger services ended on 17

The last relic of Lord Willoughby's railway: the weigh office at Edenham, later used as a farm store.

October 1871. Goods were carried in horse-drawn wagons until July 1873, but ceased soon after, following, according to one report, the death of a horse in an accident on the line. It was the end of Lord Willoughby's Railway.

A Tudor Station for Bourne

The line that caused the demise of Lord Willoughby's railway was the Bourne and Essendine, incorporated in August 1857 and opened in May 1860. Just under 7 miles (11km) of single track served Braceborough Spa and the village of Thurlby between the junction at Essendine and its terminus in Bourne. A halt was later added at Wilsthorpe Crossing. From its opening, the line was operated by the GNR for 50 per cent of the receipts, although that was raised to 60 per cent when traffic failed to meet expectations. It was absorbed into the GNR on 1 January 1865 by an Act of 25 July 1864, along with a number of other similar companies. With no turning facilities for locomotives, the line was always operated by a tank engine.

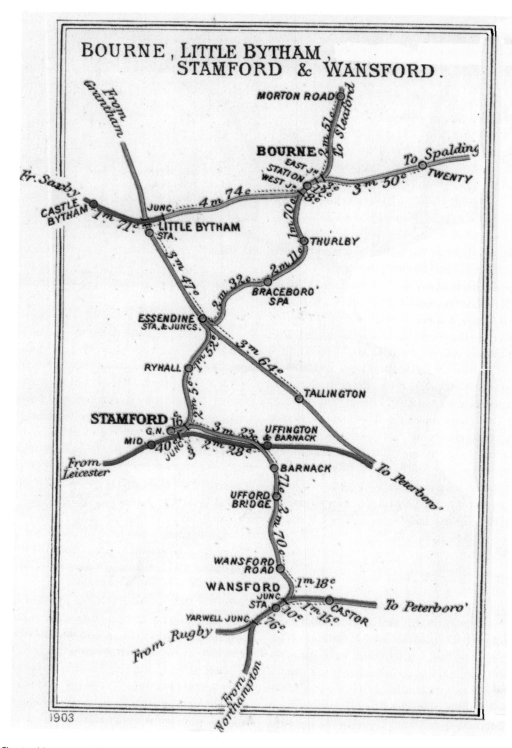

Railway Clearing House map of Bourne and Stamford connections. The Railway Clearing House shared revenues between companies based on distances travelled on individual companies' lines. Maps set standards for those distances.

Train approaching Moulton station.
D.N. ROBINSON

The most noticeable architectural feature was the fine Tudor Red Hall at Bourne, which the railway company took over as its main station building. The Hall, built in about 1605 as a country house for Gilbert Fisher, a successful London grocer, was later owned by the Digby family, although reports that it was the home of Gunpowder Plotter Sir Everard Digby are not correct.

One unusual traffic commodity was water. Natural springs at Braceborough Spa were popular with the Georgians and Victorians for their supposed beneficial effects on health – usually based on the traditional belief that if it tastes bad, it must be doing you some good! King George III was treated with it at Braceborough Hall for his 'madness' and flagons containing 5gal. (22ltr) of water were regularly sent by train to doctors and their patients in London.

Crossing the Fens

The early stages of railway mania saw many proposals come forward for lines across south Lincolnshire, linking fenland communities including Spalding, Holbeach, Long Sutton and Sutton Bridge in Lincolnshire, and Wisbech and King's Lynn over the county boundary. Many failed to be approved or built, even when approval had been received, but the Norwich and Spalding Railway, set up in March 1853, was incorporated on 4 August the same year. It had permission to build east from a junction at Spalding to Sutton Bridge, then on to a junction with another line near Wisbech. Shortage of money prevented it from building any further than Holbeach, 7 miles (11km) from Spalding, but goods services between the towns, also serving Weston, Moulton and Whaplode, opened on 9 August 1858, with passenger services following on 15 November. The GNR took on the operation of the services for the usual 50 per cent of receipts, and, following confirmation of its rights to do so by Parliament, extended the line by eight miles (13km) to Sutton Bridge, by way of Fleet, Gedney and Long Sutton, opening on 1 July 1862.

Permission was not renewed for the extension to Wisbech but, in July 1863, another company, the Peterborough, Wisbech and Sutton Bridge was authorized, with the Norwich and Spalding having the rights to operate trains over their tracks through to Wisbech. The GNR, which might have been expected to want to run this new railway, lost control to the Midland. The line opened in August 1866.

Two more elements in an east–west route, the Lynn and Sutton Bridge and the Spalding and Bourn (an older spelling of Bourne was used in the company title), obtained their Acts in 1861 and 1862, respectively, and began to build east and west from the existing lines. The Lynn and Sutton Bridge lies mostly outside the scope of this book, but one of its finest engineering achievements, the swing bridge over the Nene at Sutton Bridge, is still one of the county's most important railway relics. The current bridge is, in fact, the third on the site. The

M&GN 4–4–0 and train crossing the Cross Keys bridge at Sutton Bridge. The somersault signals show the GN part of its heritage and the signal box is typically Midland. ROD KNIGHT

first was a road bridge, replaced in 1850 by one that was modified by the railway company to carry both road and rail, with trains passing down one side and road traffic the other. The modified bridge, and the line on to Lynn, opened in November 1864. The current structure, railway-built but, again, dual-purpose, replaced it in 1897.

The Spalding and Bourne ran from a junction with the Lincolnshire Loop just south of Spalding to an end-on meeting with the Bourne and Essendine at their station in that town. No conurbations of any size exist between the two towns, but stations were built at North Drove, Counter Drain and Twenty, all named after local drainage channels, and giving rise to the old joke of 'How many stations are there between Spalding and Bourne?', to which the local will reply 'Two and Twenty'.

A proposal was soon made that the two companies should merge to form a new venture, the Midland and Eastern, which would lease the N&S and build a link on from Bourne to meet the Midland at Saxby. The GNR opposed the move, but suggested that the Midland should instead have running rights over the Bourne and Essendine and

J6 64231 with pick-up goods at Twenty station 28 February 1959. E. MEARS

Stamford and Essendine to complete the link. That was agreed, and an Act of 23 July 1866 formalized the arrangement with a 999-year lease of the N&S to the new company. The section from Bourne to Spalding opened on 1 August 1866, completing a through-route to the Midlands from south Lincolnshire and north Norfolk.

The Big Boys Take Control

Under a second Act, passed in August 1867, the GNR and Midland agreed to work both lines jointly. The overall operation traded as the Bourn and Lynn Joint Railway and was run largely as a separate company with nominal oversight from the joint operators. Formal amalgamation took place on 12 July 1877.

Beyond Lynn to the east, a similar operation was going on, with a number of small companies building short sections of track until, in August 1882, they were amalgamated into the Eastern and Midlands Railway Company. Later in the same year, the Midland and Eastern, and Peterborough, Wisbech and Sutton companies were incorporated into the Eastern and Midlands, taking effect from 1 July 1883.

The final link in the system, a direct way from Bourne to the Midland at Saxby, came about after a bill was proposed in 1888 for the Eastern and Midlands (E&M) to build a new line from Bourne to a Midland branch near Cottesmore. The Midland would then take over the whole system as far as King's Lynn, and the E&M would direct traffic towards that company's routes. Not surprisingly,

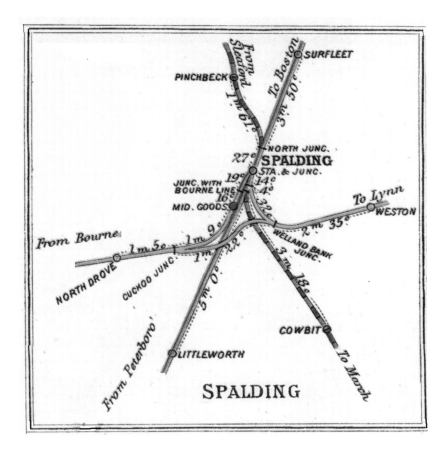

Railway Clearing House map of Spalding.

M&GN locomotive no. 91 waits with its train at Spalding station. The loco was one of a batch of 12 GNR class J3s supplied new to the M&GN. R.K. BLENCOWE

the GNR took unkindly to the idea and wiser counsels prevailed. The traffic proposals were omitted, and the Midland undertook to build the line, with the GNR having the option of linking to the Towns Line at Little Bytham.

At this point, the E&M hit a financial crisis. It was in debt to the tune of over £100,000, had taken on too many financial commitments and could not pay its way. The company manager, a Mr Read, was appointed receiver, despite shareholders blaming Read's management for the losses. The obvious solution was for the whole system to be taken over, and the Midland started discussions, but eventually it and the GNR took joint responsibility. A suggestion that the Great Eastern, which had absorbed the Eastern Counties, should be included was opposed by the GNR. A payment of £1.2 million was made to shareholders, partly in cash and partly in shares, with a further £150,000+ paid for locomotives, rolling stock and other assets. The necessary Act was passed in June 1893 and, from 1 July, most of the system was transferred into the new Midland and Great Northern Joint Railway, managed by a committee of the two owners' representatives.

The Eastern Counties Becomes Great, but Stays Eastern

The Eastern Counties Railway ceased to be on 7 August 1862, when it was incorporated into a new larger grouping, the Great Eastern Railway (GER), which came to dominate East Anglia. Like its predecessor, the Great Eastern found itself with a major trade in agricultural produce, but a great shortage of that most vital railway commodity, coal.

The principal sources were the coalfields of South and West Yorkshire and the East Midlands, where Nottinghamshire and Derbyshire were already well established and Leicestershire was being developed as a new source of both coal and iron ore. The Midland, the Great Northern, the Manchester Sheffield and Lincolnshire and the London and North Western competed strongly there, which left Yorkshire coal producers feeling at a disadvantage. That, plus the logic of the earlier proposed routes to the north, made Yorkshire the most promising target for the new GER. Unfortunately, that meant it had to run straight across territory very firmly under the control of the GNR, who also stood to lose some of its existing Yorkshire-to-London business.

An early GER bid – the Great Eastern and Northern Junction Railway – from March to Doncaster by way of Lincoln, failed in 1864 but, the following year, it was back in Parliament again. It now proposed a totally new line – the Lancashire and Yorkshire and Great Eastern Junction Railway – from an L&YR branch near Doncaster through Lincoln to Cambridgeshire. The GNR strongly opposed the plan and it again failed in Parliament,

Marching across the Fens and over the Isle

The GNR itself had obtained permission, in the same parliamentary session, for a line from Spalding to join the GER at March, which opened in April 1867. Stations were provided at Cowbit, Crowland, French Drove and Gedney Hill, Murrow and Guyhirne, several of which suffered the usual fenland problems of either being a long way from the community they served, such as Crowland – 4 miles (7km) away – or, like French Drove, having no significant community to serve anyway. Crowland was later changed to Postland – the name of the district, but, again, not an actual community.

The company also obtained permission to complete the northern part of the Loop Line by extending the Lincoln-to-Gainsborough tracks on to Doncaster, and for a series of smaller railways that would give the GNR a new north–south route from Lincoln to Spalding by way of Honington, Sleaford and Bourne.

The new northern section of the Loop opened to traffic on 15 July 1867. It continued to make use of the MS&LR's bridge at Gainsborough, then struck north, stopping at three Nottinghamshire villages before re-entering Lincolnshire's Isle of Axholme, with stations at Haxey and Park Drain. The line from Lincoln to Gainsborough was improved at the same time, with gradients reduced, stations upgraded and some bridges rebuilt, while gradients were also reduced on the approaches to some bridges on the southern part of the Loop.

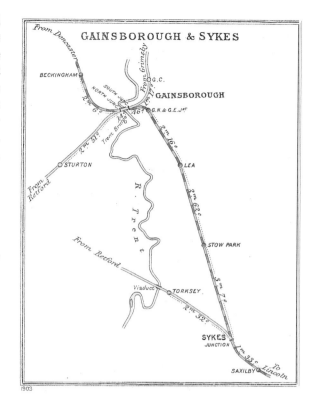

RCH map of Gainsborough and vicinity.

A Faster Way to London

The most important of the lines south of Lincoln was from there to Grantham, built as the Lincoln to Boston, Sleaford and Midland Counties Railway. Despite the long title, the line was promoted under the Great Northern Railway No. 2 Bill in November 1863, which included three separate, but linked, sections of line. The first ran along the Lincoln Edge from Lincoln by way of Waddington, Harmston, Navenby, Leadenham and Caythorpe to a west-facing junction with the Boston, Sleaford and Midland Counties at a relocated station in Honington. The second, which was never completed, although it may have been started, proposed a short north-to-east link between the two lines near Honington to allow through-running to

Leadenham GNR station, built of stone. The goods shed in the distance was brick-built. D.N. ROBINSON

Sleaford. The final section, which we will return to later, ran from Sleaford to Bourne.

The double-track line towards Grantham mostly followed the flatter lands of the clay vale to the west of the Edge, but it cut through an outlier of the higher land behind the village of Leadenham, which involved a long cutting into the hillside and a climb to the 'summit' of the line between Fulbeck and Caythorpe. There were twenty-six bridges, with most of the structures being brick-built using materials from the contractor's own works. The only major exception was Leadenham station, which local landowner Lt-Gen. Reeve insisted should be built of stone to match his Leadenham Hall. Even there, the GNR managed to sneak a cut-price element through since the goods shed fell just outside the parish, and was built in brick.

The line opened on 15 April 1867, although a special excursion loaded with local and national dignitaries travelled the route the previous day, stopping only for a sumptuous cold buffet with wine in the specially decorated goods shed at Caythorpe station. It proved to be a valuable addition to Lincoln's ways south, cutting the best time to London from over four hours by way of Boston and Peterborough to less than three-and-a-half by way of Grantham.

One important traffic commodity was iron ore, extracted from mines and quarries in the edge of the Lincolnshire Heath. Leadenham, Fulbeck and Caythorpe all saw standard gauge or narrow tracks laid from the station into the ore fields, with records showing work going on from the 1880s up to just after World War Two, although extraction at most sites had ended before World War One.

A Difficult Courtship

In view of the GNR's adamant opposition to a totally new GER line through Lincolnshire, it was becoming increasingly obvious that if the GER was to get its coal line to the north, it would have to work with its rival; but acceptable terms proved hard to come by.

The GER had obtained running powers from Spalding to March, and the GNR's Gainsborough-to-Doncaster section had been constructed in the expectation of a new joint section being built between Spalding and Lincoln. That plan was scotched in 1866 by GER shareholders, who objected to the cost. Agreement between company managers was again reached in 1867, but differences about traffic rights held by other companies prevented it going into effect. There were a number

Billingborough station in the 1920s.

of proposals for mergers between the two companies, but terms could not be agreed, so the GNR pushed on with the final part of its alternative southern route, that from Sleaford to Bourne. It was authorized at the second attempt in June 1865, but progress was slow, and the company tried to abandon the project three years later, but the Board of Trade refused to agree.

It required very little in the nature of engineering works, with the exception of a low six-arch viaduct and a fine three-arch bridge between Horbling and Billingborough, and was built for just over £100,000, of which £30,000 was for the construction of the line. Running for 18 single-track miles (30km), from the Boston line at Sleaford, it served stations at Aswarby and Scredington, Billingborough and Horbling, Rippingale and Morton Road before joining the Bourn and Lynn just east of Bourne station. It was inspected in December 1871, and passed, subject to a connection with a ballast pit being taken out and shelters completed at the two junctions and at Billingborough, the largest community between the

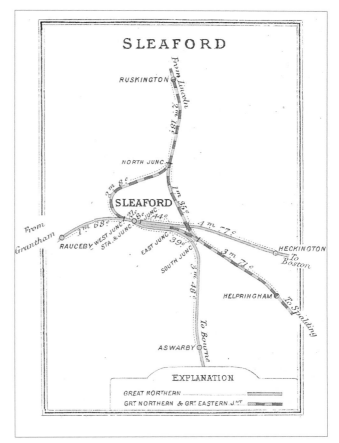

RCH map of Sleaford junctions.

The GN&GE station at Donington Road. ROD KNIGHT

towns. It was also the only one where the station was close to the village, although it was intended to serve Horbling, a mile away, and the old market and coaching town of Folkingham, something over 3 miles (5km) distant. Goods trains ran between Sleaford and Billingborough from October 1871, but the line opened throughout, and to passengers, on 2 January 1872.

The Joint Line is Born

Another attempt by the GER to break through to the north in its own right ended in 1871, when the Coal Owners' Alliance (London) Railway, heavily backed by South Yorkshire mine owners, was lost before Parliament in 1871. It would have been a joint M&SLR/GER operation from Long Stanton in Cambridgeshire up through Lincolnshire to join the MS&LR at Market Rasen.

Following another attempt at a GNR/GER merger in 1876, both companies independently proposed lines from Spalding to Lincoln the following year. The schemes went to Parliament in 1878 and, following a great deal of back-room negotiating, the GNR plan was given approval. The GER was to have full running powers and a new company would be jointly owned by its two parents, with five directors of each serving on a Joint Committee, controlling all the lines from Huntingdon, by way of St Ives, March, Spalding, Lincoln and Gainsborough to Black Carr junction, just south of Doncaster. The only new sections were to be from Spalding to Lincoln and an avoiding line, built round the south and west of Lincoln to reduce potential congestion in the city, both to be built to standards suitable for a heavy goods line. The GER was to build across the Fens from March to Ruskington, with the GNR taking on the heavier construction work over the Lincoln Heath further north. The GNR did, however, benefit to the tune of about half-a-million pounds, the calculated greater value of its contributions to the new organization.

North of Spalding, the line left the Lincolnshire Loop at Spalding North Junction and ran virtually

GN&GE Joint station staff at Ruskington. Date not known. D.N. ROBINSON

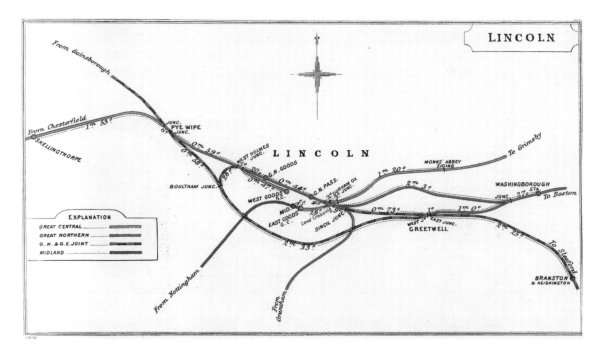

RCH map of Lincoln area junctions.

level to Sleaford, with stations at Pinchbeck, Gosberton, Donington Road and Helpringham. Twenty-one over-bridges and one viaduct were required, and the line suffered the usual bane of fenland routes – a large number of level-crossings, including the delightfully named Golden High Hedges and Blue Gowts. The tracks of the new Great Northern & Great Eastern Joint Railway (GN&GE Joint) did not pass through Sleaford, but the town was provided with spurs to the north and south, to allow trains to stop without the need to reverse back to the main line. The station, like that at Spalding, was rebuilt to allow for the increased traffic.

From Sleaford the line continued through Ruskington, Digby, Scopwick and Timberland, Blankney and Metheringham, Nocton and Dunston, Potterhanworth – or Potter Hanworth, according to the GE – and Branston and Heighington, to Greetwell Junction, where it divided into the new Avoiding Line and one that joined the GN's Lincolnshire Loop line at Pelham St junction before continuing into Lincoln Central station. The Avoiding Line re-joined the northern Loop at Pyewipe Junction. An additional link was put in place between Greetwell Junction and the Loop at Washingborough Junction to allow goods traffic from the Loop to avoid the station and level-crossings in the centre of Lincoln. Another link, from Boultham Jct brought traffic down from the Avoiding Line into the GN's goods yards. The southern section, to Ruskington, opened in March 1882 with the rest following in August, although passenger services did not make use of the Avoiding Line until March of the following year.

The Great Eastern finally had its coal line to the north, and it is generally believed that it did better out of the deal than the GNR, but both companies gained by this new, better engineered and faster north–south route through Lincolnshire.

A New Port for the Wash?

Although the GNR had not shown a great deal of interest in developing the port facilities at Boston, it did get very enthusiastic about a plan to build a totally new facility on the Nene at Sutton Bridge. In 1880 and 1881, it invested £55,000 into a £180,000 scheme to enclose 13 acres of water into a new dock. A branch was laid from Sutton Bridge station and the dock was equipped with the most up-to-date facilities. It was expected that coal from Derbyshire and Nottinghamshire would be exported to Europe, with imports flowing to the Midlands.

The first boat to enter the dock, the Garland, carrying a cargo of timber, passed through the new lock with some difficulty on 14 May 1881. The embarrassment of realizing that the lock had not been dredged deeply enough, so some of the cargo had to be unloaded before the boat could pass through, was nothing to what followed. The waters in the enclosed dock, rather than staying level as the tides went out, fell, indicating that the structure was leaking. No good reason could be detected but, on 9 June, several sections of the walls collapsed, leaving only the concrete facings. Train-loads of stone and earth were brought in to fill the gaps, but the erosion continued. It soon became apparent that the silt deposits on which the dock had been built were being washed away, leaving the structures unsupported. The situation was hopeless, and the whole project was abandoned.

The M&GNR links through to the Midland

Further west, the M&GNR built their link from Bourne to Little Bytham, with the Midland taking it on to meet their own tracks at Saxby. This removed the need for the circuitous and mostly single-track route through Stamford, across the GNR's Towns Line at Essendine and on to Bourne. The line was double-track, with the M&GNR section leaving the Bourne-to-Essendine branch and climbing at 1:100 to Toft Tunnel. From there it dropped down, across a viaduct, over the route of the old Edenham branch, and on to Little Bytham. Facilities were provided there for a junction with the GNR, but these were not taken up. The Midland then built the rest of the line, with stations at Castle Bytham, South Witham and Edmondthorpe and Wymondham. Construction was complete by May 1883 and goods services began on 5 June, but passengers were not carried until July 1894.

Building an occupation bridge over the M&GN near Saxby in the early 1880s. The men are using a derrick to hoist bricks and stones onto the construction while a Whitaker crane excavator works below. FROM 'BUILDING A RAILWAY', BY STEWART SQUIRES AND KEN HOLLAMBY

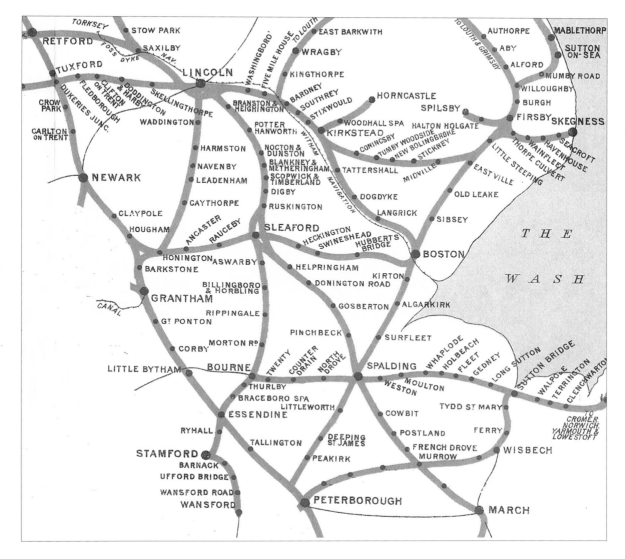

By the turn of the nineteenth century, the GN had control of, or an interest in, virtually every railway in south Lincolnshire.

The M&GNR itself, despite the financial troubles at the time, had also built an avoiding line to bypass Spalding station. As with Lincoln, these tracks were mostly used for goods in the early days, although holiday traffic from the Midlands to Norfolk would become more important in later years. The rails ran from Cuckoo Junction on the Spalding-to- Bourne Line, and passed over the GNR Loop and the GN&GE Joint before re-joining the M&GNR at Welland Bank.

With the completion of the two joint lines, south Lincolnshire's railway system was now virtually complete, but much more was happening in the north of the county.

CHAPTER 6

Ships, Steel and the Seaside

They Do Like to be beside the Seaside

While the Great Northern was backing lines that increased its hold over central Lincolnshire, the Manchester, Sheffield and Lincolnshire Railway was consolidating its presence in the north, developing a major industrial centre and beginning a new venture, which the GNR would soon follow, of serving the county's seaside resorts.

The company's first big task, though, was to implement its plans for the port of Grimsby. Although the initial 'main line' served the Humber ferries at New Holland, with passengers having to change for Grimsby, the MS&LR saw the town, and the planned new docks, as a key destination in north Lincolnshire. The Grimsby Dock Company, which had agreed to amalgamate with the Great Grimsby and Sheffield Junction on 7 October 1845, announced its intention to start work on new docks the following day, appointing an engineer and resident engineer a few weeks later. The old Grimsby Haven Company had improved the existing harbour earlier in the nineteenth century to create what later became known as the Old Dock, but more space and better facilities were urgently needed. The new dock would offer an extra 20 acres of enclosed space, as well as a 13-acre tidal basin. Two locks would give access from the Humber for

vessels up to 300ft (90m) long and 70ft (20m) wide – much larger than could be accommodated in the existing space.

Construction was formally launched by Prince Albert on 18 April 1849, although excavation had already been going on at the site for some time.

The new dock opened for business on 27 May 1852, and received further royal approval in October 1854 when the royal yacht, with Queen Victoria on board, arrived there from Hull. Her Majesty graciously agreed to it being named the Royal Dock in honour of her visit.

In the same year, authorization was given for the construction of a 6-acre fish dock, completed two years later, to provide increased accommodation for the increasing number of boats based in the port. The railway companies actively encouraged the use of the docks, with the MS&LR, GNR and the Midland forming the Deep Sea Fishing Company and the MS&LR and the South Yorkshire part-owning the Anglo-French Steamship Company. The MS&LR bought out the other shareholders in the shipping company in 1865, having taken powers the previous year to run services to north European ports, including Hamburg, St Petersburg and Stockholm. The services established played a major role in transporting migrants from Russia, Scandinavia and eastern Europe to the United States.

ALBERT AND THE DOCKS

Prince Albert, with his keen interest in industry and trade, saw the developments at Grimsby as being beneficial to both, and the MS&LR encouraged his involvement in the project. His first visit was to lay the foundation stone for the first lock into the new docks.

The Prince spent the night with Lord Yarborough before departing for the event from Brocklesby station, where the railway had provided His Lordship with his own private waiting room. His train was headed by locomotive no. 65, now renamed *Prince Albert* in his honour, as far as the dock gates, then hauled by 100 navvies 'in short white smocks and nightcaps' to where the stone was to be laid. This was hardly a single-brick and trowel-of-mortar job, since the stone was 8ft (2.5m) long and weighed 11 tons (11,000kg). There was, though, a specially designed silver trowel, although records do not survive to suggest how large it was. After completing his duties, the Prince joined 1,000 guests for lunch in a specially erected pavilion. He praised the company for creating 'a place of safety, refuge and refitment for our mercantile marine' and referred to his day's work as 'laying the foundation of a great commercial port'. He then completed what was almost a Grand Tour of Lincolnshire's railways by departing by way of Louth, Boston and Peterborough on the ELR and the GNR Loop. The navvies in their smocks and nightcaps were rewarded for their haulage efforts by a gift of £50. Albert returned three years later, on 18 March 1852, for another banquet to celebrate the completion of the

Prince Albert arrives at Brocklesby station to take the train to Grimsby. ILLUSTRATED LONDON NEWS

work. This was held in a marquee put up in the larger of the two lock chambers, and lasted four-and-a-half hours. There were fifteen toasts, including a final one to 'the Press', which probably ensured favourable coverage of the event!

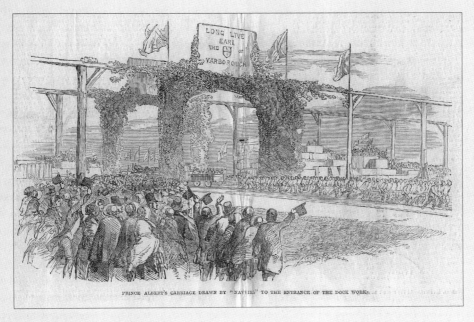

Albert's carriage 'drawn by 100 navvies in short white smocks and nightcaps'. ILLUSTRATED LONDON NEWS

Contractors building the Alexandra Dock at Grimsby in 1880.
NORTH EAST LINCOLNSHIRE LIBRARY SERVICE, LOCAL HISTORY COLLECTION

The MS&LR continued to expand the maritime facilities in the town: it now owned the Old Dock and had improved the facilities there; the fish docks were enlarged in the 1860s; a new Union Dock was commissioned in 1873 and opened by the Prince and Princess of Wales six years later. The Old Dock was enlarged substantially in 1880, and the new complex named the Alexandra Dock, in honour of that same royal visit, and a second fish dock was built and opened, then expanded further until it covered 16 acres of water by 1894.

To serve all these facilities, the MS&LR and GNR – but mostly the MS&LR – laid about 80 miles (130km) of track, built three stations, two locomotive depots and a large number of goods sheds, warehouses, cattle docks, coaling quays, sidings, loading and unloading resources, as well as that symbol of Grimsby docks to this day – the Italianate Dock Tower housing the hydraulic systems to operate the dock gates.

Looking back from the end of the nineteenth century, the company could claim, with some justification, that it had found Grimsby 'in the depths of despair' but had raised it to 'a high pitch of exultancy' by recovering 'all of and more than its ancient prosperity'. The *Illustrated London News* would no longer need to comment, as it had done in 1849, 'Many of our readers, not ill-versed in the

Grimsby Dock station. D.N. ROBINSON

Railway coal drops in Grimsby docks with the Dock Tower in the background. NORTH EAST LINCOLNSHIRE COUNCIL LIBRARY SERVICE, LOCAL HISTORY COLLECTION

geography of foreign lands, may pause here and ask where is Great Grimsby?'. Thanks largely to the efforts of the MS&LR, who had 'the wisdom … of executing the Dock works upon a scale which would render it a first-class shipping station', that question had become redundant.

New Centres to Serve

In addition to developing the rail infrastructure of Grimsby, the MS&LR was also involved in two other projects in the north of the county: the creation of the seaside resort of Cleethorpes; and serving the steel industry that was developing in, and around, the rapidly growing town and industries of Scunthorpe.

Cleethorpes had been gathering a reputation as a good place to take the sea air for some years – in 1791 John Byng visited the 'Cleathorps Inn, a bathing place of a better complexion than others we have seen upon this coast' but he was not impressed by the food, the room or the locals!

The 1846 Act had granted permission for the Great Grimsby and Sheffield Junction to build on from Grimsby to Cleethorpes. That power lapsed when the line was not built, and new proposals in 1856 failed to get approval, but an application in 1861 succeeded and the line opened on 6 April 1863. It was an immediate success – on 3 August of the same year a meeting of Primitive Methodists in the town brought 30,000 visitors by rail, including many who had crossed by packet-steamer from Hull to Grimsby, then continued on the train. A further 10,000 arrived on foot or in horse-drawn vehicles. Since the resident population of Cleethorpes at the time was in the order of 1,000 people, it was presumably something of a strain to keep them all fed and entertained. As the demand rose, new attractions were added at the resort, including a pier, opened in 1872. The increasing traffic led to the track being doubled in 1874, with an intermediate station, New Clee, opened the following year.

Not everybody was impressed. The *Gazette* took a dim view of the goings-on on Good Friday 1872:

Drunkenness stalked the streets. Men, women and boys and girls and even children – ragged and forlorn – were drunken and sickened with drink. Brutalising language, and free fights, bruised features and oaths of intoxicated girls who could not steady themselves from contact with doorways.

Taking Cleethorpes in Hand

The MS&LR remained content to serve this growing trade up until 1880, when it decided to rebuild the station to deal with the traffic. The company was then asked by the local Urban Sanitary Authority to help reduce the erosion of the cliffs, which were being badly damaged by winter storms. MS&LR

The original Cleethorpes station then and now. A service to Manchester Airport might surprise the promoters of the GG&SJR!
TOP IMAGE: NORTH EAST LINCOLNSHIRE COUNCIL LIBRARY SERVICE, LOCAL HISTORY COLLECTION

agreed that, 'provided that the land required be given or sold at nominal rates', they would build suitable defences, convert the land 'into a place of recreation, with baths and waiting rooms' and extend the station to a point closer to the main attractions on the front. The company also took over the pier, built swimming baths, installed electric lighting on the promenade, laid out gardens and provided a large number of other facilities for the visitors. A public opening was carried out with all the usual pomp and circumstance by Prince Albert Victor, one of Victoria and Albert's children, in July 1885. In total, it is estimated that they spent over £100,000 on land acquisition and other works, but gained handsomely by it, since visitors continued to flock to the resort at up to 30,000 a day on holiday weekends.

Trade to the coast was also increased by the completion of the MS&LR's other large project in the area – the opening of a new line to serve the steel town of Scunthorpe and to provide a shorter route to the industrial centres of Yorkshire.

Rabbit Farming

When the railways of Lincolnshire began to be built, in the late 1840s, Scunthorpe barely existed. It was just one of five small villages with a combined population of just over 1,200 at the 1851 census. The area was mostly poor-quality, sandy land, although rabbits had been farmed in several large warrens from the seventeenth to the nineteenth centuries.

All of that changed in 1859, when Rowland Winn, the son of a local landowner, discovered large deposits of ironstone. The first batch of ore, mined in 1860, was carried first by cart to Gunness Wharf on the Trent, then later by rail to Keadby, on a line built by George Dawes, who owned an ironworks to which the raw material was being sent.

From Keadby, the ore could be shipped by boat on the Trent or the River Don Navigation or by rail from the other side of the river on the South Yorkshire Railway, which had opened in September 1859. The railway had been built from Doncaster to the Trent on the banks of the Navigation, which it owned. Stations in Lincolnshire were Medge Hall, Godnow Bridge, Crowle – later renamed Crowle Central – and Althorpe with Keadby.

Rowland Winn's ambitions extended well beyond just mining iron ore. By 1862, he had persuaded the Dawes brothers to establish a local ironworks, and set up the Trent, Ancholme and Grimsby Railway (TA&GR), to build a line from the Trent to the MS&LR on its approach to Grimsby. Coal for the furnaces could be brought in more cheaply and processed iron sent to industrial

Crowle station alongside the South Yorkshire Navigation. NORTH LINCOLNSHIRE MUSEUMS SERVICES

areas in the north and exported from Grimsby. To achieve that end, he had to negotiate with both the MS&L and the South Yorkshire Railway (SYR), who must have had hopes of extending their line into this potential new market. Deals were done, involving special rates for SYR and MS&LR traffic, both of whom then invested £30,000 in the project, with the SYR agreeing to build the necessary bridge over the Trent.

The Trent, Ancholme and Grimsby Railway Bill received the Queen's assent on 22 July 1861, but, since most of the line crossed land owned by Winn, work was already well under way by this time. The route ran for 14 miles (22km) from a junction with the MS&LR at Barnetby, close to that of the Lincoln and Gainsborough lines. As originally planned, a 900yd (800m) tunnel would have been dug through the ridge west of Scunthorpe, but that was changed to a deep cutting with a long viaduct climbing towards it.

The only other significant obstacles were the Ancholme River and Navigation, which had to be bridged, plus earthworks at Santon and Wrawby. Engineer Charles Bartholomew was in charge of building the line, and suffered all the usual problems: land was not available at the right times; men vanished during the summer to work on the land, then returned when the weather turned against either farm or railway work; materials and equipment were often unavailable when needed; and money remained a constant source of concern, with Winn and his representatives keeping a close eye on the costs.

Traffic Troubles on the Trent

The biggest problems came from the bridge over the Trent, which was still a commercial river serving Gainsborough and other inland ports, who did not want traffic interrupted by a new bridge. Bartholomew's design was 484ft (150m) long, with a 160ft (50m) pivoting section, which required a number of piers to support it. The fears about a navigation hazard proved well-founded. During construction, several collisions involving vessels

MS&L Scotter Road viaduct at Scunthorpe. All but the arches over the road were later filled and embanked. NORTH LINCOLNSHIRE MUSEUMS SERVICES

The first bridge over the Trent at Keadby, built for the Trent Ancholme and Grimsby Railway. NORTH LINCOLNSHIRE MUSEUMS SERVICES

on the waterway took place, which, inevitably, the boatmen blamed on the obstacles and the engineers put down to bad navigation.

The work was completed by May 1864, when a special train crossed over, but the inspector required modifications to reduce the shipping hazards. The first goods train ran on 1 May 1866, with the first passenger service on 1 October. The TA&GR had also been failed in the same inspection, and £40,000 had to be spent on improvements and track doubling before opening at the same time as the bridge. Stations were built at Frodingham, still seen as a more important location, but later

Passengers disembarking from a GC train in Scunthorpe. NORTH LINCOLNSHIRE MUSEUMS SERVICES

renamed Frodingham and Scunthorpe, and at Appleby and Elsham.

Winn's aim of seeing Scunthorpe develop as a major centre for iron, and later steel, served by its own railway, was fully realized. The first iron was tapped from the Dawes' Trent Ironworks on 26 March 1864, but they were rapidly followed by others. A total of ten furnaces were in use by 1877. A short branch line, the Santon branch, was added in 1872 to gain access to another ore source.

Iron ore being loaded into a train of wagons for the Crosby Ironstone Company. Steam excavators were introduced into the mines just before World War One. NORTH LINCOLNSHIRE MUSEUMS SERVICES

Nude, Rude and Savage

The MS&LR eventually incorporated both the SYR and the TA&GR, first leasing them and then formally taking them over in 1874 and 1882, respectively. In addition to a substantial increase in goods traffic, the MS&LR also gained by greater passenger numbers heading for Cleethorpes, although the newcomers were criticized for 'nude, rude and savage scenes' when they did not make proper use of the bathing huts.

The success of Cleethorpes led to other communities on the Lincolnshire coast looking for better connections. Like its northern counterpart, Skegness had seen more visitors in search of a healthy dose of sea air. The Vine Hotel opened in 1770, and a regular omnibus service linked the town to Boston, where coaches could be met. The vital bathing machines were in operation within a few years to ensure public decency. A small shipping trade also made use of the town, but the coal and timber that arrived were unloaded over the beach rather than through any purpose-built facilities. Almost next door to Skegness, though, was the long-established, but much run-down, port and market town of Wainfleet, and early railway proposals were more interested in trade than in tourists.

Aerial view of Cleethorpes station, believed to have been taken in 1904. D.N. ROBINSON

The Lincoln, Wainfleet Haven and Boston Railway, proposed in 1845, was another of the over-ambitious railway mania schemes. It planned to build new port facilities at Wainfleet through which exports would flow from the industrial Midlands and the north, but a number of other schemes had similar ideas. Negotiations between them resulted in a proposal for a line from Lincoln to Wainfleet, but lack of money and poor planning saw it founder in 1846.

The opening of the East Lincolnshire Railway in 1848 offered a much cheaper and simpler connection, and a meeting at Wainfleet in August 1868 'unanimously agreed' that a line from Firsby to Skegness by way of Wainfleet would be 'most desirable'. As submitted to Parliament, the initial plans were just to serve Wainfleet, and passed as the Wainfleet and Firsby Railway (W&FR) without significant opposition on 13 May 1869. The Great Northern agreed to run the new line for 60 per cent of the takings. The first sod was cut in Wainfleet just under a year later, with the line opening for goods on 11 September 1871. A month later, a train

'freighted with a goodly number of passengers' left the town at 6.45am accompanied by 'a salute of detonating signals', but a full celebration was made a week later when flags were flown, the Horncastle band played in the streets and a grand firework display concluded the event.

It seems likely that the W&FR always intended to move quickly on to Skegness, since proposals for an extension were submitted within a fortnight of the initial line opening, with the Act secured on 18 July 1872. The complete line opened on 28 July 1873, with stations at Thorpe Culvert – Lincolnshire's drainage heritage once again being used to name a station – Wainfleet, Croft Bank and Cow Bank. The latter two, both again named after drains, were renamed Haven House and Seacroft, respectively, in 1900.

Unlike Cleethorpes, Skegness never saw significant investment by the railway company other

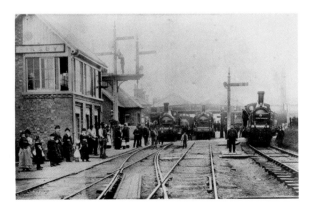

Firsby station in July 1883 the first day of services to Skegness. The trains in the left picture were ready to depart for Skegness, Boston and Spilsby. MRS SCOTT

than in the immediate infrastructure of track and stations, but the town had a similar level of support from Richard Lumley, the 4th Earl of Scarbrough, who owned most of the land there. His Lordship, acting through his agent H. V. Tippett, arranged for a new town to be laid out, and took a leading part in companies that built pleasure gardens, a pier, swimming baths and sports grounds, as well as installing water supplies, drainage systems, places of worship and a school. In return for allowing visitors free use of many of the new attractions, the Great Northern paid the Scarbrough estate one farthing (¼d or 0.1p) for every excursion ticket sold to Skegness.

The Great Northern bought out the W&FR in 1895, paying just over half a million pounds for the company, and began to improve the service and facilities. Skegness station was rebuilt and enlarged to allow room for up to 2,000 people to wait under cover for trains. Longer platforms would, according to the *Skegness Herald*, 'enable officials to load over 6,000 people at any one time, and despatch

LOCUSTS IN EGYPT

Lord Scarbrough wanted to see Skegness develop as a residential centre, rather than as a place for day visitors, and as late as 1878 *The Bazaar Office* magazine was describing it as 'a quiet, health-giving resort, not without certain charms'. However, the introduction of bank holidays in 1871, which gave working men and their families the chance for a day at the sea, made that market a very attractive one. The line opened just in time for the 1873 August Bank Holiday, and by the following year it was estimated that 10,000 visitors arrived on that day, to a town of less than 1,000 people, with none of the Earl's new attractions planned, let alone open.

The sheer numbers involved strained the abilities of the railway and the local population. The local press referred to how they left the town 'as bare of nutrients as Egypt after the visitation of the locusts', as well as the usual comments about the 'impropriety' of their bathing habits. The single-line connection to Firsby left the railway struggling, with the last of the 20,000 visitors on the August Bank Holiday in 1882 not getting away until 2.30am the following morning. It could have been worse – requests for even more excursions had been turned down for lack of rolling stock.

One shareholder complained about the delays of up to six or seven hours and GNR Chairman Lord Colville admitted that they had been 'overtaken by the traffic upon that day':

Though we got the people to Skegness all right, we could not get them away like clock-work. But I am happy to say that that enormous traffic was conducted without any accident. Some people, no doubt, were rather later in getting to bed than usual; but it was a beautiful day, and no doubt they all enjoyed themselves very much.

The peaks were the problem: in that one month just over 11,000 ordinary passengers travelled to Skegness, but the excursion traffic was more than four times as large at 47,000 people.

Probably the most famous publicity image of Lincolnshire. John Hassall's 'Jolly Fisherman' as used by the GNR to promote Skegness. NATIONAL RAILWAY MUSEUM/SCIENCE & SOCIETY PICTURE LIBRARY

twelve trains in rapid succession'. The ability to do so was further eased in 1900 when the tracks were doubled at a cost of £62,000. Skegness Urban District Council was well aware of the benefits of the railway to the town. Despite regularly nagging the company to reduce fares and introduce new services, its chairman, Councillor Rowley, told the *Skegness Herald* that 'the interests of Skegness and the Great Northern Railway are identical'.

Other coastal villages in Lincolnshire offered the potential for development as resorts. A line from Alford on the ELR to Mablethorpe had been proposed as early as 1864, and an Act was obtained, but lack of financial support prevented it going any further. The idea came back in 1871, when the Louth and East Coast Railway obtained financial support and parliamentary backing for lines that would serve three of the coastal watering places and the farming communities on the Lincolnshire Marsh. The movement of cattle from the rich pastures of the Marsh to the markets at Louth and further afield was seen as a valuable potential source of revenue. The main line was to run from Louth to Mablethorpe by way of Saltfleetby, from where a branch would serve Saltfleet and North Somercotes. The Great Northern again agreed to

run the line, in this case for twenty-one years, in return for 50 per cent of the revenue.

The Act was passed on 18 July 1872, but construction did not commence until September 1875. A second Act was required in 1877 to give the company more time, and to allow more land to be acquired at Mablethorpe for a larger station. The line opened on 16 October 1877, but the branch to Saltfleet and North Somercotes was never started.

The Alford Tramway

A proposal in 1873 to reinstate the Alford-to-Mablethorpe plan made it to Parliament, but was rejected. However, in 1880 a tramway was authorized to run between Alford and Sutton-le-Marsh, a name later changed to Sutton-on-Sea since, according to the local paper, the original title 'was not likely to commend itself by name to the holiday-maker or pleasure seeker'! This 5-mile (8km), 2ft 6in (75cm) gauge line was laid along the roads between the two towns, serving a number of smaller villages en route. It opened on 2 April 1884, after inspection by Major-General Hutchinson, and was very successful for some years, reputedly carrying 100,000 passengers in

Alford and Sutton Tramway tram in 1885. D.N. ROBINSON

1885. Return fares of a shilling (5p) for adults and sixpence for a child made it a cheap day out by the sea, and a half-day return could be had for ninepence (4p). Goods and livestock were also carried, with coal costing threepence a mile and a cow two shillings for the whole distance.

It was intended to extend the system southwards towards Skegness, but competition from a new railway line rendered the whole system uneconomic, and on 7 December 1889 the *Lincoln Gazette* reported that 'The Alford & Sutton Tramway have ceased to run their cars, ostensibly for the winter months, but really for an indefinite period.' A local paper described it as 'a melancholy event'.

The line that caused its demise was the Sutton and Willoughby Railways and Docks Company, authorized, despite the opposition of the tramway, on 28 July 1884. The docks in the title were to be built at Sutton, and were approved in the North Sea Fisheries, Harbour and Dock Act. This was another small line with large ambitions. At the cutting of the first sod in August 1885, the local paper noted the prospective benefits of 'a great port for North Sea fisheries' and the provision of a 'new, and

much needed health resort' for those suffering the 'high pressure artificial life of large towns' in the Midlands. The line would, therefore, commend itself 'as well to the capitalist as the philanthropist'. Unfortunately for the capitalists, the docks were never built and, for a time, the GNR refused to operate the line in their absence. Eventually, they agreed to do so, at the same 50 per cent of receipts as had been established with the Louth and East Coast Railway (L&ECR) for the same 21-year period, with the L&ECR lease extended to match that of the S&W. The five-mile (8km) line opened on 23 September 1886, although a full service did not commence until 4 October.

A 2-mile (3km) extension to meet the L&ECR in Mablethorpe was authorized almost immediately, despite the opposition of the tramway, over whose tracks it would need to cross. The location retained a small hut with the name of Tramway Crossing, long after the tramway itself passed into history. The extension into Mablethorpe opened on 14 July 1888, creating the Louth, Mablethorpe and Willoughby Loop. Grimoldby, Saltfleetby and Theddlethorpe were served by stations between

The first train to Sutton-on-Sea in September 1886. The locomotive was constructed in 1866 as a 2–4–0 but later rebuilt as a 2–2–2 single. Relegated from main-line duties to Lincolnshire lines, it was withdrawn in 1901. ROD KNIGHT

The station at Sutton-on-Sea.

D.N. ROBINSON

Louth and Mablethorpe, with Mumby Road the only stop from Willoughby to Sutton.

Another large-scale scheme that looked to connect with Sutton-on-Sea was the Lancashire, Derbyshire and East Coast Railway (LD&ECR), which hoped to build lines linking the manufacturing districts of the north and the East Midlands with ports on both the east and west coasts of England. The east coast outlet was to have been the planned docks at Sutton, served by a direct line for Lincoln. We will hear more about the LD&ECR later, but for now suffice it to say that it never got anywhere near the east coast.

The Lincolnshire coast was now well served by railways, although it is interesting to speculate as to whether some of the other watering places might have become better known if more lines had been built. Saltfleet and North Somercotes lost out when the L&ECR failed to build its approved extensions; and again in the 1890s, when the Saltfleet Light Railway, to run from Cleethorpes to Saltfleetby through the two communities, did not get parliamentary approval; and again in 1897 when an alternative scheme under the same name got approval but no finance.

Further south, poor shipping channels into Boston led to a whole series of plans in the 1860s and 1870s to build lines out to Frieston Shore, where a deep-water channel would allow new docks to be built. The Boston Ocean Dock and Railway Company was formed in 1891, but met opposition from Boston Corporation. They had reached agreement with the local drainage authorities to straighten the Haven and dredge a channel through to new docks in the town. The Corporation proposals were approved, and Frieston Shore never got its docks or its line. It is, however, unlikely that Frieston would have become a holiday venue, unless mud bathing had suddenly become more popular than sandcastle building.

Railway building did not end in Lincolnshire in the 1880s, but those lines that were built later tended to be for a specific purpose in a particular part of the county, and were part of the process of learning to live with the lines.

CHAPTER 7

Living with the Lines

By the 1890s, the novelty of railways had worn off in Lincolnshire, and the local population was getting used to the new facilities and services offered by this new form of transport. Those market towns that had good rail communication gained over those where a horse-and-cart was the fastest transport available, although the situation was complicated by shoppers and traders now having a greater choice of venues, so might choose to go to a larger centre than their local town. In the early years of the twentieth century, the Great Central Railway (GCR) was offering special market-day tickets to Lincoln from many of its stations in the north of the county, as well as from Hull, where the ticket included the ferry trip to New Holland.

An indication of the effect that the railways had on the price of commodities was shown in Grantham, where there was indignation when the GNR decided not to sell coal themselves in the town, which meant the locals had to pay two shillings more a ton for that delivered by canal. However, competition worked the other way for the GNR when, in 1852, it tried to double the price of parcels from London to Gainsborough from 9d to 1/6d. Local traders promptly switched to the MS&LR and other services. The change was reversed six weeks later.

Many businesses continued to thrive in small communities by taking advantage of the ability to make new connections. Records from Thurlby station near Bourne as late as the 1950s show a horse dealer having animals transported there from all parts of England and Wales. Seed potatoes, beet pulp for animal feed and fertilizers came on the train, as did timber for the owner of a local wood-yard. Churns of milk from dairy farms were collected daily, and many head of cattle, sheep and pigs went by rail to market.

Opportunities also existed for the development of new types of traffic. Fish from Grimsby was an obvious example, but the overnight movement of 4,000 lobsters from the town to London was a little out of the ordinary. Lincolnshire could claim

Thurlby station with GN type somersault signal. DAVID CREASEY

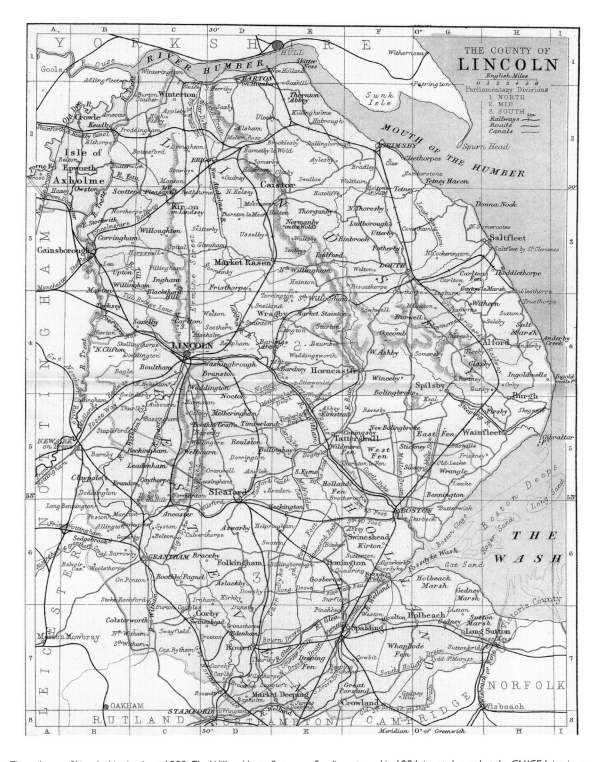

The railways of Lincolnshire in about 1883. The Willoughby-to-Sutton-on-Sea line, opened in 1884, is not shown, but the GN/GE Joint, in use by 1882, and the Bourne-to-Saxby extension of the M&GN (1883) are included.

The station (ABOVE) and goods yard (BELOW) at Spalding. The venerable tractor on the left suggests a date pre-World War One.
STUART GIBBARD

a major role in one of the great culinary developments of the late Victorian era – fish and chips – with the fish from Grimsby supported by large numbers of wagon-loads of potatoes heading from the Fens to the industrial cities of London, the Midlands and the north.

Spalding became a major centre for agricultural traffic, with the growing trade in potatoes supplemented by a big growth in the flower and bulb businesses. Daffodils, tulips and other blooms were dispatched every evening in the season to be available in the city markets the following morning.

Lincolnshire's great engineering businesses continued to thrive alongside the railways. Companies such as Marshall's and Edlington's at Gainsborough; Clayton and Shuttleworth, William Foster, Robey & Co., the Lindum Plough Company, Ruston, Proctor & Co., and others in Lincoln; Blackstone & Co. in Stamford and Richard Hornsby & Sons in Grantham had all grown dramatically since the early days, and all benefited from the proximity of railway lines, which allowed raw materials to be brought in and large, heavy machinery taken away for delivery to customers. Clayton's and Ruston's developed even closer links with the railways, as they went into the manufacture of rolling stock and locomotives for home railways or for exports, while Ruston excavators were a key tool in railway construction in later years.

Loading flowers at Spalding station.
STUART GIBBARD

Unwillingly to School?

The coming of the railways also assisted in the improvement of the education of children. The Education Acts of 1880 and 1891 had enforced free compulsory schooling on children up to the age of ten, but the expansion of secondary education in the early years of the twentieth century created new transport needs. Catchment areas for secondary schools could be large in counties like Lincolnshire, but trains made the journey shorter, if not more acceptable, to the reluctant child 'creeping like snail, unwillingly to school'. Rail journeys were not always taken unenthusiastically, since schools and Sunday schools took the opportunity to have their outings to Skegness, Cleethorpes or other more distant places.

Beyond the immediate locality, having a railway in your vicinity could quite literally give access to a world of transport and travel. Posters on tiny Lincolnshire stations promoted travel to great events all over the country or to overseas locations, such as Paris, Hamburg or the Rhine. We cannot know if anybody from the county was among the crowd of 100,000 who travelled by train to see the execution of John Wilson in Liverpool, but as early as 1851, the GNR sent 160 carriages with 4,000–5,000 passengers from Doncaster and Lincolnshire to the Great Exhibition in London.

As we saw earlier, farmers in Lincolnshire saw great benefits to the coming of the railways, since stock, produce and commodities could be moved much more quickly, cheaply and easily; but there was some resentment about their effects on the availability of labour. The railways not only made it easier for men to move away from an area in search of work, but they also provided an attractive alternative for bright young men. In 1900, nearly two-thirds of a million people – about 5 per cent of the population – worked for the railways and the numbers were rising. Railwaymen were well-respected members of the community, with the great benefit over agricultural workers of security of tenure in their jobs. Albert Simms, who left school in about 1870 to work on the land as a lad for about

'Portable' steam engines for the army being dispatched from Robey's in Lincoln about 1900. STUART GIBBARD

eight shillings (40p) a week, moved to the GNR at Boston later that decade, eventually becoming a foreman platelayer at Kirkstead, where he would have been earning over three times that wage. He had also been in receipt of a railway pension at the time of his death in 1930.

In addition to direct employment, the railways also supported many other jobs and businesses. A classic example might be the employees of W. H. Smith who manned the station bookstalls all over England, or the many people who transported goods and passengers to their final destinations. The omnibus drivers who conveyed passengers from Kirton Lindsey station 'to all parts of the town' were as dependent on the railway as was any of its staff.

Both railway employees and the public had to learn new accountabilities – the care for their own and others' safety. Railways in the early days were not only prone to accidents and mechanical failure, the speed and weight of a travelling train meant that anyone, or anything, that got in its way was likely to come off second-best. Many people took too little notice of the famous 'forty shillings' fine imposed for trespassing and walked on railway property, only to come into conflict with a passing train.

Sadly, railway lines also offered new options for people who wished to take their own lives. Joseph Birkett, the son of the Wilsthorpe crossing-keeper on the Bourne-to-Essendine line, died from 'horrific

SMART YOUNG MEN WANTED

In 1874, the Great Northern was obviously keen to recruit more from the local areas, since it sent out a note to stationmasters and others looking for 'smart active young men' to train as porters, but its standards were high. Applicants had to be at least 5ft 6in (168cm) tall, not less than 21 years old, but not more than 30, unless previously employed by a railway company, in which case up to 35 was acceptable. He had to be able to read and write, be 'generally intelligent' and 'free from any bodily complaint'. High moral standards and previous employment records were also investigated.

> The Candidate must produce testimonials of character from employers for the past four or five years, and one from each of two housekeepers of undoubted respectability; and if he has been in any public service, also a certificate of good conduct during such employment.
>
> (GNR recruitment notice)

Such employment came with responsibilities. Most staff were uniformed, and discipline was similar to that in the armed services. An employee could be instantly dismissed, or even taken before a magistrate, for a breach of company rules.

John William Winter left school at nine, and joined the Great Northern as a track worker in about 1910. He became a level-crossing keeper at Kirkstead in 1915, where he also worked the swing bridge over the river. According to his son, his philosophy of life was that if you had a clean pair of boots you could go anywhere. Photo taken in the 1930s. DAVID WINTER

injuries' in August 1870, when he lay on the railway track in front of a train near Thurlby station.

Great Dreams Realized

Despite such drawbacks, railway construction continued in Lincolnshire, although the new lines were mainly extensions to, or links between, existing systems. The MS&LR, in particular, had a very busy time around the turn of the century, both in Lincolnshire and outside the county. Away from our territory, the principal project was the new main line through the Midlands to London, and the change of name from the MS&LR to the much grander Great Central.

In Lincolnshire, though, the biggest work was the establishment of another large port complex at Immingham, just north of Grimsby. Immingham had been considered by the MS&LR, back in the 1870s, as an alternative to adding more docks in an increasingly crowded Grimsby, but the company preferred to stay within the existing complex at that time. However, when more space was needed at the turn of the century, the company backed the Humber Commercial Railway and Dock. The new company obtained parliamentary approval on 9 August 1901, but land was obtained at Immingham before making the proposals public. The backing, by what was now the Great Central, was initially unpopular in Grimsby, although inquiries

Great Central loco no. 428, an 1877 design by Sacre for the MS&L. Seen near Market Rasen on a Lincoln-to-Grimsby train. BRYAN LONGBONE

made by the Corporation and others rapidly overcame the opposition. A second, more detailed, bill was withdrawn when a House of Commons committee, and various public bodies, inserted clauses that would have made the scheme impractical and uneconomic. Negotiations with the Board of Trade resulted in the removal of some of the more onerous conditions and, following agreement by the GCR to lease the new complex for 999 years, an Act was passed on 22 July 1904.

The sod-cutting ceremony took place two years later, despite a massive thunderstorm that damaged the marquee and disrupted all the arrangements. Excellent work by the caterers and others got things back in order, although it was reported that GCR staff, acting as stewards, found their top hats had filled with water during the storm.

Lady Henderson, the wife of the GCR's chairman, Sir Alexander Henderson, was cheered as she performed the necessary digging, or perhaps for her adroitness in wheeling the sod along a gangway for disposal! The usual round of toasts and celebrations followed before a steam-powered mechanical excavator, often referred to as a 'steam navvy', began removing the soil from the new dock site.

The new facility covered a thousand acres of land, much of it reclaimed from low-lying marsh, with the dock itself occupying some 45 acres. A number of new railway lines were constructed to serve it, with the first being the Grimsby District Light Railway. This was built under the terms of the Light Railways Act 1896, which did away with the expense of obtaining a parliamentary Act and allowed a company to plan and build a line, with just the requirement for a more easily obtained Light Railway Order. The line could be built to lower technical standards than a conventional railway, providing maximum speeds of 25mph (40km/h) – or less on bends! – were maintained.

The new line, first proposed in 1902 but not authorized until 1906, was planned to connect with the Grimsby street tramway system, but that connection was never installed. It eventually ran from Pyewipe Road in Grimsby to the dock estate, with a link from the main Grimsby-to-Sheffield line provided by a modification of the existing Great Coates dock branch. The Great Coates link opened first, in 1906, and the line was initially mainly used by contractors at the new dock, but demands for a public passenger service led to the Grimsby connection being put in in 1909 and a steam railcar service introduced from January 1910. The trip took twenty minutes and cost the first-class traveller a shilling (5p) return, with the third class paying half that – 6d – and workmen just 4d.

The second new line was the double-track Humber Commercial Railway, connecting the docks to the Grimsby–New Holland line just north

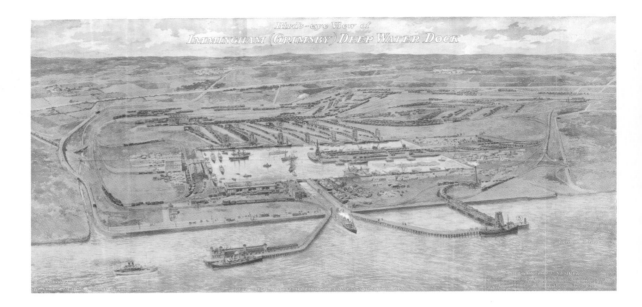

Promotional material for the GCR's new dock complex at Immingham. *ROD KNIGHT*

of Ulceby station. This served both jetties to the north and south of the main dock complex and initially opened in an incomplete state in January 1910, possibly for the use of the contractors. It was fully operational by May 1912 and became the main goods access to the facility.

The third link was created by the Barton and Immingham Light Railway, planned to run directly between the two communities, probably with ambitions to continue along the Humber shore to join up with lines planned further west, but later reduced to a link between Immingham and the existing Grimsby-to-New Holland Line near Goxhill. The line opened in two stages, but was completed in May 1911, serving Killingholme, Admiralty Platform and East Halton en route. Provision was made for double track to be laid, but it remained single track throughout its existence.

A Big Business Gets Royal Support

The Great Central was now in control of another major transport hub, incorporating: the rectangular dock basin; two miles of quays and berths; two deep-water jetties, one of which housed a passenger

Steam railmotor at East Halton station. BRYAN LONGBONE

terminal; a 6-acre timber pond; two grain eleva-tors and six hydraulic coal hoists, each served by eight sidings. There were four large transit sheds, a warehouse for grain and one for wool and a bonded store. The whole complex incorporated some 170 miles (270km) of track, with the ability to handle over 17,000 wagons at a time. It was served by a thirteen-road engine shed with repair and coaling facilities, a water-softening plant and dormitory facilities for locomen away from their home depots. Such an investment deserved a proper opening cer-emony, which it received on Monday 22 July 1912, when His Majesty King George V and Queen Mary arrived to do the honours, even though the docks had already been in operation for two years.

The royal party arrived just after noon, ironi-cally in the Great Northern's Royal Train, to be met by Sir Alexander Henderson, Sam Fay, its general manager and a bevy of local dignitaries. The King and Queen then toured the new docks on the paddle steamer *Killingholme*, while the train, hauled by GCR locomotive no. 364 *Lady Henderson*, was moved into position.

Once the Royals were back on dry land, speeches and presentations were made, culminating in a request by Sir Alexander that the new dock should be named 'the King's Dock'. The request was 'gra-ciously granted', after which, to the great surprise of almost everybody present, Sam Fay was called onto the dais and knighted on the spot as Sir Sam Fay. It

was reported that the enthusiastic cheers could be heard 6 miles (10km) away in Grimsby.

Despite the massive expenditure and effort that went into the Immingham project, the GCR did not neglect Grimsby. An Act was passed in 1912, which should have led to a third fish dock being completed there, but the intervention of World War One led to the proposal being shelved, although it was suc-cessfully revived in the 1930s.

The increasing traffic from the new docks and the iron- and steelworks at Scunthorpe led to improvements to the permanent way on the Grimsby-to-Doncaster lines. Tracks were quad-rupled along the choke point between Wrawby Junction and Brocklesby Junction; Barnetby station was substantially rebuilt, and the signalling along the stretch was improved, with five new signal boxes installed between the two points.

Further west, the swing bridge at Keadby was by now severely out of date and needed to be replaced. After fighting off a number of other bridge propos-als promoted by rival railway companies, approval and local authority support were obtained for a 550ft (170m) combined rail-and-road bridge. This incorporated a 160ft (50m) Scherzer rolling lift span, giving a much larger clear passage for ship-ping than the previous structure. Two fixed spans over the river and two approach spans completed the structure, which required a 2-mile (3km) devia-tion of the lines and the building of new stations at

The 'new' King George V Bridge at Keadby, opened in 1916. JOHN FOREMAN

THE CLICKETY

Grimsby and Immingham Electric cars at Corporation Bridge. JOHN MEREDITH

Interior view of Grimsby–Immingham tramcar. JACK RAY

In addition to what might be described as the conventional railways serving the two communities, an additional passenger link was created when the Grimsby and Immingham Electric Railway opened in May 1912. Known locally as the 'Clickety', it was an overhead electric tramway similar to some American inter-urban systems running for most of its route alongside the conventional tracks of the Grimsby Light Railway. Authorized as part of that system, it inherited its powers to make a connection to the town tram tracks. Unfortunately, delays in rebuilding Corporation Bridge in the town, which the line would have needed to cross, prevented the connection being put in. Eight passing places were provided along the single line, which ran for just under 6 miles (10km) from the bridge to the docks. Powers were provided to allow the line to continue into Immingham itself, which would have been a popular move in both communities and a source of useful additional revenue, but although part of such an extension was built, it never came into revenue use, resulting in the line failing to make the best possible connections at either end.

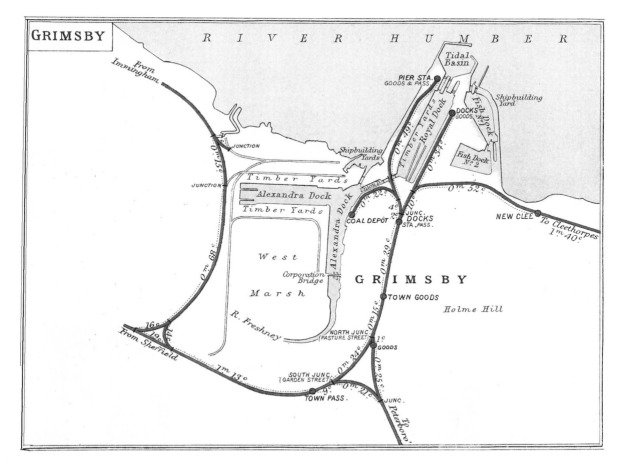

RCH map of railway connections in Grimsby.

Althorpe, replacing one of the same name, and at Gunness and Burringham. Building began in 1912 and was completed, as the King George V Bridge, in May 1916. According to one report, the driver of the first train over the old bridge travelled, at the age of 76, on the footplate of the initial service over the new one.

'As Mad a Scheme as Ever Presented to Parliament'

Further south in the county, the Great Central also eventually absorbed the rump of what had been planned as the Lancashire, Derbyshire and East Coast Railway (LD&ECR), despite the MS&LR having once described it as 'as mad a scheme as was ever presented to Parliament'! Its grandiose plans for a line from Lancashire to a new port at Sutton-on-Sea never got off the ground, but a line into Lincoln from the west did open in December 1896. The more ambitious plans were foiled by a lack of funds, and although they got financial support from the Great Eastern, keen to obtain access to the East Midlands' coalfields, the help was conditional on dropping the other parts of the larger scheme. The line was opened in two parts. The first, from Edwinstowe in Nottinghamshire ran to a connection with the GN&GE Joint's tracks at Pyewipe Junction, just west of Lincoln, while the rest, from Edwinstowe to Chesterfield in Derbyshire, was

Rowlands Sidings signal box alongside the Fossdyke Navigation near Pyewipe Junction. PETER GREY

Midland Railway Johnson 4—4—0 'coupled bogie' locomotive no. 2185 at St Mark's station in Lincoln in 1908. LINCS TO THE PAST, REF LCL 83

completed in 1897. The line crossed the Trent on the long Fledborough viaduct, consisting of 59 30-foot (9m) brick arches on the western approach and four 110-foot (35m) steel spans over the river itself. The company only built one station, Skellingthorpe, in Lincolnshire, although Clifton on Trent and Doddington and Harby were both on the county side of the Trent and served communities here. Pyewipe Junction, and the goods yards associated with it, was to become a busy centre of railway activity in Lincolnshire, with the added attraction for the staff of easy access by boat across the Fossdyke Navigation to the Pyewipe Inn, which had given its name to the location.

No Tunnelling under the Cathedral

The LD&ECR relied heavily on connections with other lines, entering Lincoln by courtesy of one company and continued to the coast thanks to another – the MS&LR/GCR were only too glad not to face a competing port in Lincolnshire and offered favourable terms to coal traffic carried from the East Midlands through Lincoln to Grimsby. A separate company, the Lincoln and East Coast Railway and Dock took over the rights and powers

east of Lincoln, including the possibility of a tunnel passing almost underneath the cathedral, but never got beyond parliamentary approval.

The London connection, by way of its links with the GE, was also attractive to other railways operating in the East and North Midlands, and the LD&EC established working arrangements with the Midland and the MS&L that allowed services to operate to Sheffield and Mansfield as well as to collieries in the area. Connections to the GNR Towns Line at Tuxford and to one of its other lines at Langwith Junction brought more coal traffic, but passenger business on the route remained low, although vigorous attempts to promote the line as 'the Dukeries Route', serving many of the stately homes and the attractive countryside in the area, did succeed in attracting some tourist traffic.

Dividends were paid to shareholders for a short time, but none were received in the twentieth century. The small size of the company made significant improvement unlikely, so, despite opposition by some board members, including those from the GER, ownership was offered in 1905 to the GNR, who turned it down. The Great Central rapidly put in an offer of £1,000,000 plus meeting the costs of the necessary parliamentary approval and laying in whatever junctions might be needed between the companies' lines. The offer was immediately accepted and the LD&ECR became part of the Great Central on 1 Jan 1907.

Low-Cost Lines in the North

The MS&LR/GC was also involved in, or affected by, two smaller railways built in the north of Lincolnshire at the turn of the nineteenth/twentieth century. Both were given an initial impetus by the previously mentioned Light Railways Act 1896, designed to be particularly useful to people wanting to build inexpensive lines in rural locations.

The Axholme Joint Railway (AJR) was a combination of two such railways in this rich agricultural area. Several lines had been proposed earlier, including the Isle of Axholme and Marshland Tramway, authorized in 1883. This was taken over by the MS&LR, but not built. Another scheme, the Goole and Marshland Light Railway appeared a few years later, but was held back by its supporters once it was realized that the Light Railways Act was on its way, and could cut their costs. Brought back as the Goole and Marshland Light Railway, it was approved by the Board of Trade in 1898 to run from the North Eastern Railway's Goole-to-Doncaster line across the Isle to Fockerby on the Trent. Another scheme, the Isle of Axholme Light Railway (IoALR), left Reedness Junction on the G&MLR, and went south by way of Crowle, where it crossed the Great Central's tracks to Scunthorpe, and on through Epworth and Haxey to Haxey

The first sod being cut at Epworth for the Isle of Axholme Light Railway on 20 July 1899. NORTH LINCOLNSHIRE MUSEUMS SERVICES

Junction on the GN&GE Joint. A branch ran from Epworth to Hatfield Moor. Both lines were approved under a single order in 1899, although construction of the G&MLR had already begun in September of the previous year. The IoALR carried out its own sod-cutting ceremony on 28 July 1899.

The first section, to Reedness Junction, opened on 8 January 1900, and a trial excursion by a special train carrying G&MLR directors onto as-yet unopened IoALR tracks took place in June, followed by a trip to Epworth in December. Neither of the founding companies ever worked as an independent organization, since operation was initially carried out by the North Eastern Railway. It and the Lancashire and Yorkshire Railway were keen to take the businesses over, which they did in 1902

The Directors of the Goole and Marshland Light Railway on a visit to the works of the IoALR at Crowle.
NORTH LINCOLNSHIRE MUSEUMS SERVICES

Crowle station on the AJR. D.N. ROBINSON

First train into Winteringham on the NLLR. NORTH LINCOLNSHIRE MUSEUMS SERVICES

to create the Axholme Joint Railway. Once the joint company was formed, the whole line was worked by the L&Y, which had more convenient locomotive facilities than those of the NER.

Passenger traffic on the northern lines started in August 1903, with goods on the whole system inaugurated on 14 November 1904, following the completion of the biggest engineering challenge on the line – the embankments, viaduct and bridges south of Crowle. These included a swing structure over the South Yorkshire Navigation and a girder bridge over a road and the GCR line. An inspection by the Board of Trade was required before the AJR could open throughout to passengers, but this was carried out on 9 December, allowing full operation to begin on 2 January 1905.

On the other side of the Trent, the Great Central saw the AJR line to the Trent as a potential L&Y/NER crossing into Great Central territory, and a potential threat to their lucrative goods traffic from the mines and steelworks on the east side of the river.

It had supported the approved, but not constructed, Trent Valley Light Railway in 1900, but saw another opportunity soon afterwards when a local landowner, Sir Berkeley Sheffield and others, with interests in the ironstone deposits, proposed the North Lindsey Light Railway (NLLR), a line from Scunthorpe north towards the Humber.

With financial backing from the GCR, the NLLR opened its first 6 miles (10km) from Frodingham to West Halton on 3 September 1906. A further stretch to Winteringham was being served by 15 July 1907 and Whitton, on the Humber bank on 1 December 1910. A very basic terminus there served the town and the thrice-weekly Hull-to-Gainsborough packet-boat. A short branch from Winteringham to Winteringham Haven created a link to a jetty from where a ferry ran to Hull on Mondays, returning on Wednesdays.

A station at Winterton and Thealby was added later, as was a goods depot at Normanby Park. An extension was considered from Winteringham to Barton-upon-Humber, where it would have created a loop with the GCR's Barton branch, but was never built. The line did, however, serve the GCR's purpose in blocking incursions by the AJR or its owners.

New Attempts to Cross the Trent

The Lancashire and Yorkshire, in particular, promoted several schemes, including the very ambitious Ackworth and Lindsey Railway of 1904. This would have run from Ackworth, in Yorkshire, across the Isle of Axholme and under the Trent before linking the NLLR with North Killingholme, Barton and Grimsby. Electric traction was to be used, but opposition by the GCR and the NER, protecting their interests in Hull, blocked the plans.

The L&YR returned to the fray in 1906, with an unsuccessful scheme to extend the AJR from Fockerby over an eight-arch bridge to Alkborough, from where the NLLR would carry the traffic to Winteringham, where new port facilities would have been built.

Another plan for a road/rail bridge over the Trent was put forward in 1909 but got no further than the planning stage following the approval for the new Keadby bridge for the GCR. The NLLR and the AJR then settled down to relatively quiet rural and mining existences, respectively.

A Quicker Route to the Sea

Ever since the rise in holiday traffic to the coast, the Great Northern had been looking for a way to shorten its route from Lincoln to Skegness and the other resorts it served on the Lincolnshire coast. The need arose because trains from the city and beyond had to continue down the Loop Line to Boston and reverse there to go back up to Firsby or Willoughby to connect with the branches. We have already heard about the suggestion that the Horncastle and Spilsby branches could be linked by tunnelling through the Wolds, and a number of other proposals, dating back as far as 1883, were put forward, but it wasn't until August 1911 that the *Railway Magazine* could report a final decision:

Holiday resorts on the Lincolnshire coast, and Skegness in particular, are becoming increasingly popular, and in order to provide quicker means of communication between the populous centres of the West Riding and Skegness, the Great Northern Railway company has decided to build a new railway 15 miles long. The new line will commence about 1½ miles south of Kirkstead station on the Lincolnshire branch running from Lincoln to Boston ... joining the East Lincolnshire line where it crosses the Bell Water Drain, halfway between Little Steeping and Eastville stations. The new line means much to the City of Lincoln, as Skegness will be reached in about 45 minutes, as against 2 hours by the existing route via Boston. It will also be of

immense advantage to the inhabitants of numerous villages who are at present placed at great disadvantage as regards railway communications. The lack of railway facilities is more seriously felt by the agricultural community, and farmers will reap considerable benefit from the new railway.

The line was approved on 27 December 1911 as the Kirkstead and Little Steeping Light Railway, but seems to have been universally and practically known locally as 'the New Line'. It was easily constructed over flat farmland, with the main obstacles being the fen drains that crossed its path. Three road-bridges, one over and two under, were required, as well as a brick bridge over the River Bain at Coningsby. It is reported that the building of the line only required the demolition of a single house. Goods traffic began on Sunday 1 June 1913, with the first passengers carried a month later on Tuesday 1 July.

The 'numerous villages' referred to above did undoubtedly benefit, but although Coningsby, New Bolingbroke and Stickney were reasonably sized communities, the others, at Tumby Woodside and Midville, were very small. The line's main *raison d'être* was to hurry trippers to the coast. Despite that, the locals were enthusiastic. The Rev. G. H. Hales bought the first ticket to be issued at Stickney, declaring his intention to have it framed for posterity; a lady from New Bolingbroke carried a banner to Coningsby reading 'The Good Times Have Come'; and a number of tickets to Skegness were sold with the proviso that the passenger could go first to Kirkstead before riding back over the whole of the line before continuing from Firsby to the coast.

As per the Light Railway regulations, trains on the line were initially limited to 25mph (40km/h), but since the tracks had been laid to full main-line standards, that was soon raised to 50mph (80km/h). That may well have been reduced again within a short time of its opening, since one track of the double track was lifted in 1916 to allow the rails to be shipped to the Western Front during World War One as part of the British war effort. Unfortunately,

Timetable of trains on the New Line at the opening in 1913.

as part of the German war effort, the ship carrying them was sunk on its way to France and the rails never arrived. The full system was restored by 10 July 1923.

Kirkstead would also have been served by the Mid-Lincolnshire Light Railway, planned to run from there to Sleaford, but although an order was obtained in 1914, the GNR and the GER refused to take on the responsibility of operating it. With the outbreak of war, the idea went into cold storage, from which it never reappeared.

Naval Fliers Take to the Rails

The last 'full-scale' railway constructed in Lincolnshire was actually built on behalf of the navy! During World War One the Admiralty had established a training camp for Royal Naval Air Service pilots at Cranwell, on the Lincolnshire Heath just south of Lincoln. Getting equipment and supplies to the base in winter conditions proved difficult so a 5-mile (8km) contractor's line from Sleaford station to the site was laid very quickly in the spring of 1916. Goods and workmen were carried, but it became

Workmen building Stickney station on the New Line. PAT BANISTER

a valuable amenity to the trainee pilots to whom it offered a route to the brighter lights of the town. Being naval staff, the train became a 'liberty boat' on which the airmen 'went ashore'. If they had known the standards of construction, they might have been less happy, since the Board of Trade refused to pass the line as suitable for passengers. The Admiralty responded that risks had to be taken in wartime, so 'obligatory peacetime standards' should not apply, and that argument was accepted. An improved line was commissioned in 1916 through the Great Northern, who owned Sleaford station, and was built by contractors Logan and Hemingway. It was in use by the following year, although ownership passed in 1918 from the Admiralty to the newly formed Royal Air Force, who established the Royal Air Force College there.

The 'Cranwell Express' was not universally popular with its passengers – the ride was rough and the carriages were redundant four- and six-wheeled stock bought second-hand from the GNR, hauled mostly by small industrial tank engines. Servicemen and others were charged three shillings and sixpence (17½p) for the trip, but a local bus company offered the trip for a shilling less, resulting in the closure of the railway to passengers in 1927. In a move that was to be echoed many times over the coming years, the bus company then raised their fare to that previously charged by the railway.

The line remained in operation for goods traffic until August 1956, although the service had deteriorated to a single train a day, weekdays only, mostly carrying coal for the base's boilers. A number of special services were run, including excursions by a young persons' charitable organization, The Crusaders' Union, in 1931 and 1938; the first contingent of Canadian trainees during World War Two and two trains for the Coronation in 1953. The track was lifted in 1957.

Mergers Denied

Lincolnshire's main railway companies – the GNR, GCR and eventually the GER – had rollercoaster

RAF Cranwell station at the College. D.N. ROBINSON

relationships, with periods of close cooperation followed by spells of bitter rivalry. In 1907, the GNR and GCR began to discuss running the two companies under a joint committee – not a full merger, but a 'close and amicable arrangement'. Both companies already had extensive running powers over each other's lines and the GCR made great use of the GNR's main line into London for many of its south-bound services.

The plans were rejected, so the two companies began working with the GER on a much larger scheme, effectively controlling large parts of eastern England and the East Midlands. A bill was put forward in 1910, but met strong opposition. Many MPs were still in favour of promoting greater competition between railway companies, rather than reducing it; the rail unions saw a risk of lower pay and fewer jobs, and rival companies were concerned about potential loss of trade. The bill did pass in the House of Commons, but was then put to a committee that was given such wide-ranging powers that it was obvious nothing would happen quickly. It was, therefore, withdrawn, although the companies carried through some of the economies that had been hoped for.

A Slightly Tarnished Golden Age

The years before World War One are often seen as the golden age of the railways, and Lincolnshire was well served by its internal lines and the connections beyond the county. Rail travel was now fast and reliable, with the 1888 and 1895 'Races to

the North' carried out by the groupings of companies who ran through trains to Scotland on what are now the East and West Coast Main Lines, demonstrating the ability of their locomotives and dramatically cutting the times to Edinburgh and beyond.

Corridor carriages were in regular use on many trains, with toilets and restaurant cars available to the passengers – the Great Northern had six-wheeled corridor coaches with lavatories in use for first-class passengers in 1881 and the provision gradually spread to lesser categories. Sleeping cars were on offer to long-haul travellers, with Pullman cars for the more affluent. Improved brake and signalling systems, in and on the carriages, improved safety, although the county did see two serious accidents in the period. The first was the Little Bytham crash of March 1896, and the other took place at Grantham in 1906.

At Little Bytham, just to the south of Grantham, a King's Cross-to-Leeds express derailed at 70mph (112km/h), while crossing a recently relaid section of track. The ballast under the rails had not been properly packed down, but the speed restriction had been removed, as had the flagmen, who should have been in place to warn the driver of the train. Six carriages were derailed, with one falling over a bridge parapet onto the road below. Two people were killed in the incident, and four more were injured. The inquiry, headed by Major Marindin, praised the bravery of the train guard, Mr Nott, who continued to help the passengers despite being injured himself.

The Grantham event was a much less straightforward affair. A King's Cross-to-Edinburgh sleeper and mail train, which had been due to stop in Grantham at 11pm, ran straight through the station at high speed. It then derailed at points set against it to allow a goods train to cross over to the line to Nottingham. The inspector's report stated that the locomotive, a GNR Atlantic, its tender and nine vehicles were wrecked, with seven of them thrown down an embankment. At least two fires then broke out among the wreckage. One sleeping car and two brake vans at the rear of the train were also derailed, but remained upright on the embankment. The driver, Fred Fleetwood, and fireman, Ralph Talbot, were both killed instantly, as were nine passengers and a post office worker in one of the mail vans. Two other passengers died later, and thirteen more, plus four railway staff, were injured.

Slow Trains and Crossed Legs

Although Lincolnshire was perhaps fortunate in avoiding more such accidents, it was less lucky in that it did not see the benefit of many of those innovations of the period. With the exception of the GNR Towns Line through Grantham, and some improvements on the GCR services in the north, the county did not greatly benefit from the increased speed of the trains.

WHAT CAUSED THE GRANTHAM ACCIDENT?

Onlookers watching the removal of the wreckage from the 1906 Grantham accident.

Wrecked carriages from the 1906 event.

The death of both foot-plate men meant that the cause of the accident remained a puzzle. The inspector considered a number of possible reasons why the train did not stop, including: mechanical failure, for which there was no evidence; the possibility that the driver was drunk or incapacitated; that he was ill; that the driver and fireman had been fighting; or that they had both forgotten that they were due to stop at Grantham, despite having been in charge of the same train the previous night. However, he failed to find good evidence for any of the suggestions and came to no final conclusion in his report:

A sudden illness of the driver appears certainly the most probable of them, but there is no direct evidence to completely substantiate any one of them; it is feared therefore that the primary cause of this accident must forever remain a mystery.

A recent suggestion is that when an extra van was added to the train at Peterborough, the last stop before Grantham, the rush to keep the train on time meant the brake pipes between the two end vehicles on the train were not attached correctly, meaning that the train brakes were not operative. This would not have been noticed on the climb away from Peterborough, and would only have become apparent as the train approached Grantham, with just the relatively inefficient locomotive brakes to stop the whole train.

The theory fits the incident well, but does not square with evidence given that the pipes were attached and the brakes tested. For it to be correct, it is necessary to assume that someone misled the inquiry, and that railway staff and officials 'closed ranks' to prevent the story coming out. That possibility is backed up by a specific instruction, issued the day after the crash, that an alternative method of releasing the train brakes, possibly used at the time, was not to be used in future. It is likely that the full truth will never be known, but the fact that the incident has not been forgotten was shown by the rededication, 100 years after the event, of the grave of Georgiana Baguley, the only crash victim to have been buried in the town.

Apart from the Towns Line, few long-distance trains originating elsewhere passed through the county, although the M&GNR ran services from the East Midlands cities to Norwich and Yarmouth, as well as many excursions to the north Norfolk coast. The Great Eastern made use of the GN&GE Joint for services between Liverpool Street and Doncaster or York, plus a daily restaurant car express from York to Harwich, on the Essex coast, where it made connection with Continental steamers to the Hook of Holland and Antwerp. Through-coaches, which had come over the GCR from Liverpool and Manchester, were attached at Lincoln.

As far as greater comfort was concerned, the fact that the GNR had to make a point of promising that excursions from London to Skegness would be with corridor coaches – which had toilets – might indicate that that was not usually the case!

An early MS&L' locomotive, 2–4–0 no. 79, built in 1849 as Acteon but rebuilt in 1886 to this condition. Seen at Oxbow Crossing, New Holland, in the 1890s, it was scrapped in 1902.
BRYAN LONGBONE

The failure of the Sutton Bridge dock scheme had lost a promising new source of goods revenue, and the developments at Immingham, although they would be of great value in the future, took some time to make an impact. However, Boston saw new docks opened with increased goods being handled, and the GNR laid a branch into the new facility to tap that traffic, although it did not contribute financially to the docks.

An agricultural recession in the 1880s and 1890s had reduced both outgoing produce traffic and demand for fertilizer and other agrarian inputs, although that had begun to improve by the early 1900s. The same conditions also affected the output of the county's engineering firms, and some went out of business. Others, though, diversified beyond agricultural machinery and expanded into the new century. Robey's went into dynamos and electricity supply; Ruston's built electrical equipment, pumps and boilers and Marshall's developed new trades in gold-dredging and tea processing. Clayton and Shuttleworth might be described as setting in motion a process that would be to the detriment of the railways when they started to build steam road wagons, as did Robey's, while Foster's produced showmen's engines that powered fairground rides and pulled the equipment from one location to

another. Hornsby's took on a series of patents owned by the Yorkshire-born engineer Herbert Akroyd Stuart and built the world's first diesel engines, several years before Rudolf Diesel produced his own version!

The railway companies served all these companies well in distributing their products all over the UK and beyond.

They Did Like to be beside the Seaside

The holiday and excursion trade continued to grow, with the coastal resorts offering all the attractions now expected – piers, rides on the sands, bathing facilities, seaside rock, tacky gift shops and deck-chairs, alongside such Victorian innovations as 'What the Butler Saw' machines, all despite stern injunctions that 'booths, stalls, swings, roundabouts, coconut shies, shooting galleries, Aunt Sallies or other erections' were not permitted. A clock tower was erected at Skegness in 1899 to celebrate Queen Victoria's Diamond Jubilee and visitors were encouraged by what is possibly the most famous railway seaside poster of all time – Hassall's picture of the Jolly Fisherman, painted for the GNR in 1908 for a fee of eight guineas, enhanced by the slogan

Holidaymakers arriving at Mablethorpe (ABOVE) and Cleethorpes (BELOW). BOTH ROD KNIGHT

RIGHT: Promotional flyer for an excursion from Leeds to Grimsby and Cleethorpes in 1870.

GREAT NORTHERN RAILWAY.

TRIP TO
GRIMSBY AND CLEETHORPES.

On SATURDAY, 24th SEPTEMBER,

A

CHEAP EXCURSION

TO

GRIMSBY & CLEETHORPES

WILL RUN AS UNDER:

FROM					TIMES.	FARE There & Back.
					a.m.	s. d.
LEEDS	dep.				6 0	
Holbeck	,,				6 3	
Beeston	,,				6 9	
CASTLEFORD	,,				6 0	
Methley	,,				6 6	2 . 6
Stanley	,,				6 11	
Ardsley	,,				6 23	
Lofthouse	,,				6 28	
WESTGATE	,,				6 33	

Returning the same day only from Cleethorpes at 6.30, Grimsby Docks, 6.40, and Grimsby at 6.50 p.m.

Children under Three years of age, Free; above Three and under Twelve, Half-fares. Tickets not Transferable. No Luggage allowed.

London, King's Cross Station, September, 1870.

HENRY OAKLEY, *General Manager.*

Waterlow & Sons, Printers, Carpenters' Hall, London Wall.

TAKING THE WATERS AT WOODHALL

One unusual resort in the county was Woodhall Spa, where the discovery of what were claimed to be medicinal bromo-iodine waters encouraged visitors in search of better health or a congenial environment. A spa was erected and four substantial hotels, the Alexandra Hospital, a golf course and a number of boarding houses were built to cater for the visitors, all to an overall plan drawn up by a London architect, Richard Adolphus Came. From 1898, the GNR offered through-carriages to and from London, which served Woodhall and the town of Horncastle, the terminus of the branch concerned. Woodhall saw, and sees, itself as a more genteel resort than its brash competitors on the coast.

GN train arriving at the Horncastle and Kirkstead Railway Company station at Woodhall Spa. Early 1900s.

'Skegness is so Bracing'. All the coastal resorts saw a variety of convalescent homes where 'visitors of a delicate health' could recuperate.

The railways were happy to run excursions from almost anywhere to anywhere. One remarkable example was provided in 1910 by the GCR on a Sunday excursion from Marylebone to Grimsby and Cleethorpes. According to the LNER magazine, that was the longest distance and cheapest half-day excursion run by any railway at that time. Starting in London at 11.05am, the distance of 223 miles (360km) was covered in 4h 39min, a stop of 8min being made at Leicester to change engines, at an average speed of nearly 50mph (80km/h). The fare of 4/3d (21p) works out at just over 8 miles (14km) for an old penny. One can't help but wonder what time they got back home again!

Visitor numbers to the county's resorts rose rapidly in the early years of the twentieth century, with Skegness seeing three-quarters of a million in 1913. The eight months to 4 August 1914 alone saw 400,000 arrive, but the trade and the golden age came to a shuddering halt that week, as the lights went out over Europe and World War One broke out.

Railways at War

The railways of Britain were to play a major role over the next four years – they moved troops,

---

ATTACKS FROM THE AIR

The railways in Lincolnshire suffered some damage from enemy action, with bombs from Zeppelin airships falling on Grimsby, Frodingham, Immingham and East Halton stations, killing a signalman at Immingham and injuring four others. One Zeppelin night-raider tried to follow a train into Lincoln, but the driver, noticing the presence of the airship, stopped his train short of the city, whereupon the attacker dropped his bombs on the village of Washingborough. No casualties were caused by the bombing, but two people drowned when an overloaded ferry-boat carrying would-be sightseers overturned on the Witham close to the village. An opportunity to bring down one of the airships was lost at Mablethorpe when, despite the machine being illuminated by a searchlight in the town, the anti-aircraft gun did not fire at it. It seems that the crew were unwilling to take action without their officer, who was drinking in a local hotel. The officer concerned then fled on a bicycle, only to be caught later in Peterborough.

---

equipment, munitions, coal for the fleet and food for the whole country.

In Lincolnshire, large numbers of troops were carried to training camps at Belton Park and Harrowby, near Grantham, with temporary branch lines laid in to serve them. Brocklesby Park was used as a training ground by the Grimsby 'Chums' – the locally recruited infantry battalion. Grimsby

Loading or unloading railway wagons of supplies on Grimsby docks during World War One. NORTH EAST LINCOLNSHIRE COUNCIL LIBRARY SERVICE, LOCAL HISTORY COLLECTION

and Immingham became important naval bases, with over 400 of Grimsby's trawlers based there being converted to minesweeping and other military work – a total of 216 vessels were lost either on such work or sunk by the Germans while fishing. Immingham's coaling facilities were used extensively by the navy, with up to nine heavy coal trains from South Wales arriving in the port in a day. It also became a submarine and torpedo boat centre, with mine-laying destroyers based there later in the war. The port lost a lot of sea-borne trade as European ports closed to its vessels, many of which were either captured by the Germans or requisitioned for war service by the Admiralty. Most became military transports, although the Humber ferries served as seaplane carriers, with *Cleethorpes* operating as far away as off the coast of what is now Iraq.

Troops were stationed in the ports and other points along the coast in anticipation of a possible German invasion, and an armoured train, hauled by a GNR locomotive, patrolled suitable branch lines in the county and in Norfolk. Receiving stations for wounded soldiers were set up at Grantham and in Lincoln, with a major military hospital in the premises of Christ's Hospital School in the city. Boston became a centre for the repatriation of sick and wounded prisoners of war who were taken from there by ambulance trains. The same route was used at the end of the war for repatriation of prisoners held by both sides.

Coal, Steel and Iron Ore

All the major engineering works in the county took on war-work, among the most significant being the transport of the first tanks from Foster's works in Lincoln for trials and later for use on the Western Front. Steel output from Scunthorpe increased and, to meet the demands of the blast furnaces there, a new line was opened into the iron ore fields south and west of Grantham. The High Dyke branch, which joined the GNR's Towns Line just south of the town, opened in 1916, but the first recorded train-load of ironstone left on 15 October 1917.

Coal trains from Yorkshire to London on the GN&GE Joint increased in number and weight, and passenger services were cut back and often heavily loaded, with refinements such as restaurant cars removed for the duration. Speed and frequency on the Towns Line suffered as more goods and troop trains took up track space. In 1914, Grantham was served by twenty-nine non-stop trains between there and London; but that had fallen to six by 1918.

Women carriage cleaners working on the GCR during World War One.
NORTH EAST LINCOLNSHIRE COUNCIL LIBRARY SERVICE, LOCAL HISTORY COLLECTION

Many railway workers volunteered for military service: overall, 10,000 GNR men – 30 per cent of the 1914 workforce – served in the forces, 1,000 of whom died, and the GCR provided similar levels of service and suffered even higher casualties. To keep the traffic moving, railway companies had to look for new sources of manpower. Women filled many of the vacant posts, although the promise by the companies to hold jobs open for the men when they returned meant that few stayed in railway service beyond the end of the war.

Post-War Problems

The railways and their staff were worked hard during the war, and by the close of hostilities, in November 1918, all the lines and equipment were suffering from a lack of adequate maintenance. The railways of Lincolnshire emerged into the post-war world in a dilapidated and shabby state. The Great Central had 112 locomotives under repair in September 1919, with 98 more waiting for attention out of a total locomotive stock of about 1,300. The dock facilities at Grimsby and Immingham needed £10,000 spending on them to bring them back to full commercial operation and dredging the

approaches to Immingham had to wait until 1922 before it could be completed. The Great Northern had seen its seaside traffic dwindle dramatically during the hostilities as excursions were at first limited, then banned altogether, and the lines that served the resorts had suffered from neglect. On lines other than the main Towns Line and the GN&GE Joint, the county continued to be the recipient of locomotives and rolling stock 'cascaded' from more profitable routes elsewhere, and the general need to keep stock in operation longer meant that some of what was running in Lincolnshire was very ancient indeed.

Wages had risen considerably during the war, while general goods and passenger traffic had decreased, and government control of the whole national system, extended for two years after the war to consider the future of the rail network, made it difficult to plan for the future. Proposals for light railways between Spalding and Sutton Bridge, and between Boston and Wrangle failed to come to fruition, although several farmers began to lay the first sections of what would later become known as the Lincolnshire potato railways, using track and rolling stock no longer needed behind the trenches of the Western Front.

Strikes by railway workers were not confined to the period after World War One but were a regular feature of the early years of the twentieth century. Police were called to Lincoln's Midland station in 1911 to protect railway property. LINCS TO THE PAST, REF LCL 440

A rail strike in the autumn of 1919 not only increased the railways' costs, it also provided a salutary demonstration of how well goods could now be carried in lorries, many of them war surplus, operated very cheaply by demobilized servicemen. A large increase in the rates for the carriage of goods, imposed by the government in 1920, and a miners' strike the following year, put additional pressure on the companies.

All Together Now

The difficulties that many of the lines were having helped drive the government towards the announcement, in 1920, that they would promote a bill that would see the whole network 'grouped' into a small number of larger, more economic companies. The idea was vehemently opposed by many railwaymen, with the GNR's chairman, Sir Frederick Banbury, MP, taking a leading role in the parliamentary opposition to the proposals. It was 'bastard nationalization', he claimed.

Initially, it was suggested that five groups would cover England and Wales, with a separate organization for Scotland and one for Ireland, still part of the UK at that time. Eventually, after a number of other patterns had been considered, it was decided that four main entities would be brought into existence, one of which, the London and North Eastern Railway, would cover the eastern side of Britain, including most of Lincolnshire's lines. The Great Northern, Great Eastern and Great Central were all to be part of the LNER, as were the Horncastle Railway, the East Lincolnshire and all the other smaller units. The exceptions were the Midland line from Newark to Lincoln, which was to be part of the London, Midland and Scottish Railway (LMSR), and the M&GNR and the Axholme Joint, which remained separate companies, jointly owned by the LNER and LMSR.

Ironically, in Lincolnshire's situation, the amalgamation brought about the combination of the three main companies that had been planned, but rejected, barely a decade earlier. It did mean, though, that most of the staff involved knew each other, to the extent that Sir Sam Fay, in his final message to Great Central workers, could sound optimistic about the future:

> I hope and believe that the amalgamation – although the change of name is a matter of regret to us all – and the enlarged company will be to the general advantage and tend to the well-being and happiness of the staff as a whole.

CHAPTER 8

Lincolnshire and the LNER

Lincolnshire's new railway masters, the London and North Eastern Railway Company (LNER), met with a variety of reactions from their staff and supporters. Within the system there was a lot of support, tempered by concerns that jobs would be lost in the rationalization. There was strong competition for senior managerial jobs, although a certain level of 'Buggins' turn', based on seniority, was inevitable, and there was a desire to see some degree of sharing out among the original companies.

Cecil J. Allen, then working for the Great Eastern, expressed 'a certain feeling of apprehension', in his book on the LNER, but concluded later that the new company was establishing 'a reputation greater than anything we had known before'. The change was obviously welcomed at Skegness, where, according to the local paper:

> When the first LNER train arrived at 6.30am they were greeted by the staff under Station Master Mountain singing 'Hail Smiling Morn'.

Many others, though, must have felt rather like George Houlden, a newly employed porter at Dogdyke station who told me 'We didn't see any difference at all until the uniform changed, and then it was just the badge'!

In many ways, George was right. As an ex-GNR man his company would still be being run from King's Cross and the line on which he worked would still serve the same communities in the same way as it had always done. Even the locomotives and rolling stock would have looked the same, since the LNER largely took on the GNR's green locomotives and varnished teak rolling stock. A parsimonious attitude to expenditure also saw paperwork from the old companies continue to be used – a report on a bombing raid on Louth in 1941 was submitted on GNR-headed paper, eighteen years after that company had ceased to exist. Seen from higher up the management ladder, things looked more difficult. The government had controlled the railways for seven years, and had handed over a system in dire need of restoration and upgrading, with wages up by 150 per cent, coal doubled in price and steel for rails hard to come by. Increasing competition from road transport, and a government desire to see prices fall at home, had resulted in passenger fares and goods transport rates only 50–60 per cent higher than those of 1914.

The situation was made much worse in 1926 by the General Strike. Normal railway services closed down for ten days, although some trains continued to be run, with 150 operating on 4 May, the first day of the action, rising to over 1,200 by its end. Most were run by non-striking staff, but volunteers also played a part, although the LNER would probably have preferred that one such in Lincolnshire had

Railway staff at Willoughby station wearing a mixture of GNR and LNER badges. Late 1920s. D.N. ROBINSON

not happened. A train from Grimsby arrived in Boston driven by a strike-breaking vicar with the help of two students. The train had taken seven hours for a journey normally run in less than two and had smashed through several sets of level-crossing gates en route!

Even after the end of the railway strike, the companies had problems with the supply of locomotive coal, since the miners stayed out for several more months. Coal was first drawn from stocks but then had to be imported. The supplies were intermittent and often of poor quality; LNER director William Whitelaw commented that the Israelites making bricks without straw in Egypt had an easier job than locomen keeping steam pressure up on the coal provided.

The General Strike is estimated to have cost the LNER over ten million pounds in reduced revenue, although costs were cut by four million, most of which would have been paid to striking workers. In addition, and probably more important, the strike had once again shown how well road transport could fill the gaps left by the railways, and at a lower price.

Depression and Closures

The ending of the strike did not raise the company's fortunes to the extent that might have been expected, since it, and the country, went straight into the Great Depression of 1927–33. The LNER suffered particularly badly, being dependent for a large amount of its business on mining and manufacturing. Lincolnshire's engineering companies, already struggling to switch back from war-time production to their usual agricultural and other machinery, saw demand fall at home and abroad. Steel output fell, resulting in less activity in Scunthorpe, and fewer coal and iron ore trains. Some improvements to track and other facilities were made, under a government plan to help the economy by reducing passenger travel duty on condition that the extra money was invested in the system. A sign of less happy times to come, however, was the decision, in 1925, to close the loss-making passenger services on the North Lindsey Light Railway; followed in 1927 by that on the RAF Cranwell line; in 1930 from Bourne to Sleaford; and in 1933 by the Axholme Joint, all to save money. The decisions were hardly surprising or unexpected. While working at Haxey in the early 1960s, I was told by one of my older colleagues that he never took the train to Epworth because he was faster on his bike, and my father told a similar tale about his father who used his pony and trap from Billingborough to Bourne or Sleaford.

In an almost unheard-of move to try to reduce costs, the entire LNER workforce, from directors

Loading potatoes at Spalding station. STUART GIBBARD

Most agricultural traffic in Lincolnshire was outbound to the rest of the country, but wagon-loads of Spanish oranges were brought to Spring's jam factory at Brigg for the production of marmalade. SCUNTHORPE TELEGRAPH

down to the engine cleaners, porters and messenger boys, took a 2.5 per cent reduction in pay, fees and wages from 1928 to the end of 1930.

Coal as a traffic commodity was causing concern to the new company. The amount being carried was falling and the export trade declining in the face of increasing competition from those same suppliers who had filled the gaps during the Strike. Total coal tonnage moved fell from 102 million tons in 1923 to 87 million two years later, and coal exports declined by over 5 million tons in 1924 alone. In Lincolnshire this meant less goods traffic on the Joint Line and reduced exports passing through Immingham.

Boost from Beet

One major new traffic commodity that was taking off in the 1920s was sugar beet, being grown in Lincolnshire and East Anglia for sugar production. The bulky nature of the commodity meant that the railways were well suited to it, and large quantities were delivered by train, as was the coal required for the boilers and many of the workers. Alf Nettam, who worked at the Bardney factory

in 1927–28, remembered six special trains for workers to and from Lincoln at the change of each shift.

The potato and vegetable businesses continued to thrive, with 300–400 wagons a day of potatoes alone leaving the county between July and April en route to city markets and to the docks for export. Sibsey and Tumby Woodside were important concentration points for potatoes, and whole trains of vans of flowers and vegetables left Spalding and other stations in the Fens. Many of these commodities had already travelled by rail before they even got to the stations, since they had been moved from the fields on the farmers' own tracks.

Fish from Grimsby continued to be important for the new company, although fish trains for London were diverted from the ex-GCR lines to the East Lincolnshire, where the 'fast fish' services became a feature of the line for many years. Fast seems to have been the operative word, since there are many references to trains supposedly limited to forty-five wagons at 60mph (96km/h) exceeding both parameters on a regular basis. The LNER also completed the pre-war plan for the new 38-acre No. 3 Fish Dock at Grimsby.

FROM THE FIGHTING TO THE FIELDS

The ending of World War One allowed an unusual set of lines to be laid down in Lincolnshire. War surplus narrow-gauge track and rolling stock from the trenches were bought by local farmers to help with the potato harvest. Since potatoes are 'lifted' at the back end of the year, ground conditions can get very difficult for horse-drawn carts, but the same horses could move steel wheels on steel track much more easily.

Light railways had been laid in the Fens to facilitate loading winter crops since before the war, with the earliest probably being those laid by George Caudwell and A. H. Worth in 1909 and William Dennis a year later, but the big expansion happened in the 1920s after equipment no longer needed at the front became available. The track came in ready-made panels that could easily be moved from one field to another as harvest progressed, so the systems usually consisted of a spine of more permanent way with side tracks laid as and where necessary.

More than fifty such railways have been identified by Stewart Squires for his book on the subject, with a total of about 140 miles (220km) of narrow-gauge track between them. Some were very short – simple lengths of panel track laid from a field to a road or farmyard, with horse-power the driving force – but others were much more extensive, covering complete systems of fields and yards, hauled by steam or internal combustion locomotives, with interchange facilities at local stations.

The largest of them, and the longest lasting, was the Nocton potato railway with 23 miles (37km) of track serving all parts of the farm, including greenhouses, a mill and the pig sties, from where the muck was loaded directly into railway wagons for distribution on the land. A gantry over the River Witham allowed sugar beet to be delivered directly to the factory at Bardney. Other major systems included Worth's Fleet Light Railway, at 13 miles (20km), which connected directly to another 7 miles (12km) owned by J. H. Thomson. Dennis's had upwards of 20 miles (32km) of track, including sidings and loops.

Most of the potato railways continued to give service to the farmers until the late 1930s or early 1940s, but a number continued into the 1950s, with Nocton not finally closing until 1969. That was not the end, however, since some of its equipment was reclaimed, first for the Lincolnshire Coast Light Railway at Humberstone and later, after that closed, as a museum and tourist attraction

Potato railway worker and horse-drawn wagon.

The Nocton potato railway interchange with the Joint Line at Nocton and Dunston.

close to Skegness. They have now carried troops, tatties and trippers and serve as an excellent reminder of the varied history of the equipment.

Frodingham Updated

Despite the difficult times for profits and investment, the late 1920s and early 1930s saw the biggest single railway development in Lincolnshire since the construction of the docks at Immingham. The railway facilities at Frodingham and Scunthorpe were woefully inadequate to deal with the requirements of the iron and steel industry, and a programme of improvements was approved by Parliament in 1925.

When the LNER took over, there were four large steel plants in the area, with all significant transport handled by rail. Into the district came ironstone,

Frodingham Trent signal box. JOHN FOREMAN

lime, limestone, coal, coke and building materials, while 'exports' consisted of finished steel, as well as pig iron and processed local ore for use elsewhere. Serving them were a large number of relatively uncoordinated sidings opening off the main line and the North Lindsey tracks, with two poorly served and located passenger stations and a goods shed badly placed to serve the needs of the rapidly growing town. All were controlled by an inefficient signalling system.

The company took the bold decision to sweep much of it away, and replace it with a planned complex of a new passenger station on a fresh site, a relocated goods depot, a fully equipped loco shed and a new yard incorporating enough sidings to hold over 1,500 wagons. To achieve this feat, the main road from Scunthorpe to Brigg was realigned over two new bridges, about a mile of the main Doncaster-to-Grimsby line was diverted, a new junction with the NLLR created and a re-signalling of the system was installed under the control of two new signal cabins.

The new passenger station, now simply 'Scunthorpe', serving both the main line and the NLLR, opened on 11 March 1929, despite the contractors having to work in a snowstorm to complete the facilities. The new road followed shortly afterwards, with the final element, the Brigg Road Bridge, opened on 28 June by Field Marshal Sir William 'Wullie' Robertson, a Lincolnshire legend who rose in the ranks from a humble private to become the Chief of the Imperial General Staff during World War One.

To handle all this traffic required a substantial loco stud, and the servicing depot supporting Scunthorpe/Frodingham also had to be replaced. Originally situated 6 miles (10km) away on the far bank of the Trent, any job at the station or in the steelworks involved a loco coming 6 miles (10km) along the main lines, adding further congestion to the already crowded tracks. It also had to cross the swing bridges over the South Yorkshire Navigation and the Trent, either of which could be blocked by water-borne traffic passing through. The water supply at the depot caused problems by having to be drawn from the Navigation, which was often contaminated by saltwater coming in from the tidal Trent.

A complete new loco depot was, therefore, constructed close to the new station, with a water supply drawn from artesian wells in the area, although they, too, proved to be contaminated, and a water-treatment plant eventually had to be installed.

The interior of Trent signal box with signalman George Calladine in September 1968. JOHN FOREMAN

The new Scunthorpe station shortly after opening in 1929. NORTH LINCOLNSHIRE MUSEUMS SERVICES

By the middle 1930s, most of the new developments were in place, meeting the increased demand for steel and steel products, as the national economy recovered, with the motor industry rapidly become a significant user of its products. A new business also built up in the transport of slag, a waste product of the steel industry, which proved very useful for road construction and repair, although the irony of the products they were carrying contributing to improvements in road transport may not have been lost on the railway company.

Slow and Unsteady

Passengers in Lincolnshire were still receiving a mixed level of service. On the Towns Line, some of the finest bogie carriages in the country made up the East Coast Joint Stock, and Pullman cars were introduced onto some of the services to Yorkshire. Speeds quickly recovered to pre-war levels on these premium services, and some semi-fast services in Lincolnshire saw improved rolling stock and better timings. The best time from Lincoln to London had been 2h 53min in 1910, which had come down to

Springbok taking a goods train up Gunhouse Bank west of Scunthorpe. The smoke from a banking loco can be seen at the rear of the train. JOHN FOREMAN

A banker, running tender first. August 1964. JOHN FOREMAN

GNR Stirling single no. 233, as modified with a domed boiler in 1899, leads a train of mostly non-bogie coaches north from Boston in 1907. *P.W. PILCHER/ROD KNIGHT COLLECTION*

2h 25min in 1922, but was only a minute faster in the 1930s. For most of the county, however, speed and comfort remained firmly at the low pre-war levels. Grimsby, which had been 3h 23min in 1914, had risen to 3h 55min in 1920 and 4h 7min by 1925. The passengers were also still 'enjoying' a basic ride. According to the July 1934 edition of the *Railway Magazine*, the LNER owned more than half of the national stock of old four- and six-wheeled, fixed wheel-base stock, and the magazine notes that many of them were still to be found in Lincolnshire. Ex-GNR six-wheelers were often slotted into the semi-fasts and provided most of the stock for the Grimsby, Louth and Mablethorpe services. GCR four- and six-wheelers served Barton-upon-Humber and New Holland, and mixes of the two companies' short stock provided the equipment for excursions from the Midlands to Skegness.

Small-Scale Steam

The Great Northern had had a brief flirtation with steam railcars before the war, two of which were used on a number of Lincolnshire services, including those between Mablethorpe, Louth and Grimsby, but all were scrapped or converted into non-powered articulated twin coaches in the 1920s. The conversions could later be found working the Horncastle and Bourne-to-Essendine

branches. Despite this lack of success, more types were later purchased by the LNER, with some manufactured by the Lincoln engineering firm of Clayton's. Clayton's had a long history of building rolling stock and steam wagons, but the combination proved difficult for them. Eleven were built for the LNER between 1927 and 1928, along with eight four-wheeled trailers, and were trialled on the Lincolnshire Loop between the city and what had been Kirkstead station, now Woodhall Junction. One, *Chevy Chase*, was based in Lincoln for a time, and worked between there and Grantham, Grimsby and Retford. All were withdrawn by 1937.

Services to the seaside did build back up again after the war. In 1930, despite being regarded as a poor year for visitors, over 600,000 arrived at Cleethorpes by train, just under half a million at Skegness and nearly 170,000 at Mablethorpe or Sutton-on-Sea. Excursions were very popular. On Saturday 4 June 1931, the Leeds and District Branches of the Kingston Unity Friendly Society had their annual outing and went to Cleethorpes. Nearly 8,000 persons made the trip with more than half of them children. The party was described in the LNER magazine as 'one of the largest dealt with in recent years at Leeds Central Station', noting that 'each train carried labels of a distinctive colour, and ribbons of a corresponding colour were worn by each child'.

The company itself helped to encourage days out. In May 1936, 14,000 visitors arrived in Cleethorpes to take a look at an exhibition of the latest locomotives and rolling stock, and LNER ships and ferries did a roaring trade out of Grimsby, with 44,000 'excursionists' carried during the summer of 1935.

The LNER also re-instated the GNR's half-day excursions to Skegness from London in 1925, using main-line locomotives and rolling stock, and all for the price of seven shillings (35p) – about a fifth of the normal return fare. Promotional campaigns in Hull, Birmingham and Nottingham saw additional visitors arrive, and figures for 1936 and 1937 show a rise of 22 per cent – more than 2,500 extra travellers – from Nottingham, 40 per cent more from Sheffield and the West Riding of Yorkshire, and a doubling of visitors from Manchester and other parts of Lancashire. That increase was undoubtedly helped by the opening, in 1936, of Billy Butlin's first Luxury Holiday Camp at Ingoldmells, just to the north of the town.

Sutton-on-Sea and Mablethorpe both recovered their pre-war excursion numbers, with the latter peaking at 166,000 passengers in 1936. The trade may not have been helped by D. H. Lawrence's reference in 1926 to 'the flat, dree coast', although he found Mablethorpe to be 'rather nice … with great

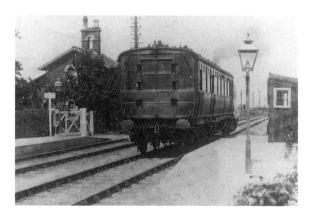

GN Railmotor at Fotherby Halt, between Louth and Grimsby. ROD KNIGHT

sweeping sands that take the light, and little people that somehow get lost in the light'.

The M&GNR was also in the business of serving the seaside, but its passenger trade mostly passed through Lincolnshire on its way to the Norfolk coast. The line remained under the joint ownership of the LNER and the LMSR, although the LNER took over full responsibility for rolling stock and

Excursion from London arriving in Skegness behind Atlantic 4–4–2 no. 4427. D.N. ROBINSON

operations from 1936. Ironically, most of its passenger traffic originated with the LMSR, coming from its heartlands of the East Midlands' cities and Birmingham, although goods were locally generated from the fields and farms of Lincolnshire and Norfolk.

Despite the railway promotions, coaches were taking an ever-greater slice of the business. On the two days of the August Bank Holiday in 1931, 44,000 passengers arrived by train but nearly 50,000 came by road, mostly in buses or coaches. In 1935, an alternative was offered to passengers from Nottingham when an air-transport company flew two flights a day into Skegness, but the service closed at the end of the summer season.

Lincolnshire's most interesting long-distance service continued to be the North Country Continental, as the cross-country express through the county was now known. The main train now left Liverpool Central at 2.20pm, arriving at Lincoln at 5.20pm. It continued down the Joint Line through Spalding to March, terminating at Harwich, reached

at 9.29pm. The 268 miles (430km) journey from Liverpool took just over seven hours, but anyone who had joined the Glasgow portion, attached at Lincoln, would have been travelling for over ten hours.

The county only suffered one serious rail accident in the period, when, on 15 February 1937, a York-to-Lowestoft train hauled by 2829 Naworth Castle derailed at Sleaford North Junction as it negotiated the points too fast for its booked stop at Sleaford. Three coaches overturned, hitting a platelayers' hut in which a five-man gang were having their midday break. Three of the gang were killed, a fourth died in hospital that evening and the fifth was seriously injured. The inspector later reported that, although there were a number of passengers in the train, 'the casualties among them were, comparatively speaking, trifling, being confined to 15 cases of minor injuries and shock'.

Road competition remained the LNER's principal problem, with goods in particular leaking away to lorries. The railway companies had always

---

FISHING FOR BUSINESS

The rivers and drainage canals of Lincolnshire were always attractive to coarse fishermen, and the railways catered to them with large numbers of special trains and excursions. For a national match held in the 1930s, six twelve-coach trains were stabled in the yard at Woodhall Junction, which would have meant that several thousand competitors and their supporters would have been spread out along miles of the river banks. Some matches were sponsored by breweries, and on those occasions the train might travel slowly down the track, which ran alongside the River Witham, with individual fishermen dropping out from an opened door by their marked spot or 'peg', then standing by the track to receive a free bottle of beer handed out from the guards' compartment as it passed by – all highly reprehensible, but very convenient. The travelling fishermen were regularly accompanied by bookmakers, who illegally took bets on the trains – betting at locations other than racecourses was banned until 1960. The bookies retired to the King's Arms at Martin Dales during the match, and paid out the winnings on the trains back again later. Local boys also benefited by collecting empty beer bottles to return. A penny for a crown cap bottle or tuppence for a screw top was a valuable addition to a lad's pocket money, as was the

Fishermen on the Witham Bank near Bardney as a north-bound excursion passes. STEVE PRIESTLEY

ha'penny he could gain by taking a fisherman's billy can with dry tea in it to the boy's home, boiling a kettle and bringing back fresh hot tea.

offered a road-distribution service for onward delivery from their stations, but local competitors were offering the same at lower prices and more convenient timings. Even that staple of the railways, potato transport, drifted away to the lorries, with the railway companies shooting themselves in the foot in the 1930s by trying to impose centralized traffic control onto a very variable and seasonal business. The requirement that farmers should be able to predict just when and how many wagons they would require and for how long was impractical and bureaucratic, so the business was lost.

Off the Rails but Still Carried by the Railways

Buses and coaches continued to be the most serious threat for passenger journeys, and the railway companies looked for ways to take some of that traffic for themselves. They had offered some road-passenger services in the past, but the legal position was complicated. A change in the law in 1928 clarified the situation, and the LNER invested over £2 million in a number of existing bus companies, although, like the other lines, it undertook not to take a controlling interest in them. In Lincolnshire, its principal interest was in the Lincolnshire Road Car Company, although it also held shares in the Eastern Counties Omnibus Co., East Midland Motor Services and Trent Motor Traction, all of which served the county to a greater or lesser extent.

Competition from other bus operators was restricted a little by the 1930 and 1933 Road and Rail Traffic Acts, which required transport companies to be licensed. The same Acts also removed some of the restrictions on the ability of the railways to offer special rates for goods traffic, although the requirement to publish rates for every commodity made it easier for competitors to undercut a price.

These benefits, and the general improvement in the economy, allowed for what has been described as the 'golden age' of the LNER – the last five years before World War Two, although it has to be admitted that many of the improvements only affected the usual corner of Lincolnshire – the stretch of the Towns Line between Essendine and Grantham!

Over that period, the LNER built a reputation based on speed and innovation. The first of Sir Nigel Gresley's Pacific locomotives had come into service in 1922, just before the demise of the GNR, but they had been making a big difference to timings on the main routes. What really caught the public eye, though, was the introduction of his streamlined 'A4' Pacifics, and their matching high-speed trains, starting in 1935. Gresley had considered following German and American practice in introducing fast, lightweight diesel units, but experiments led him to believe that a suitable streamlined steam locomotive and train could match the performance of the diesels, while carrying a larger, more economic number of passengers.

The first such set was the 'Silver Jubilee' with its four 'Silver' locomotives – *Silver King, Link* and *Fox*, plus *Quicksilver*. A trial run in October saw the 105 miles (170km) to Grantham covered in 88min, but with the remarkable top speed of over 112 mph (180km/h).

The success of the Jubilee led to the construction and introduction of the 'Coronation', a fast train from London to Edinburgh, stopping only at Newcastle. This came into service in 1936, sporting a two-tone blue livery for the coaches, which included a streamline beaver-tail observation car. The final set, also in blue, was the 'West Riding Limited' serving Leeds and Bradford.

Thirty-three streamlined locomotives were built, one of which, *Mallard*, provided Lincolnshire with its greatest moment of railway triumph, when it set the world steam speed record of 126mph (202km/h) on Stoke Bank, south of Grantham.

Cruising by Rail

Lincolnshire also featured on the itinerary of the LNER's 'Northern Belle' land cruise trains. These comprised six sleeping cars; two restaurants and a kitchen car; and two coaches that were part of the 'Flying Scotsman' set incorporating a cocktail bar and a hairdressing salon, as well as staff

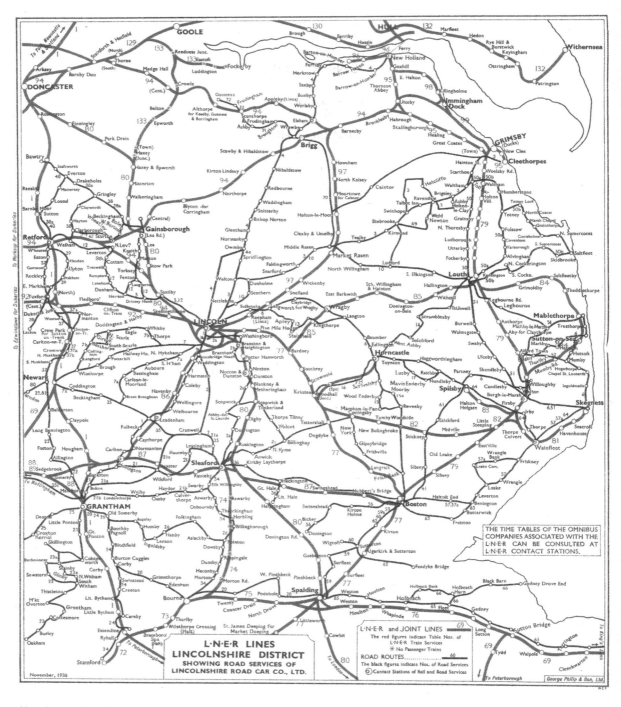

Map showing the LNER lines in Lincolnshire and the services of the railway-controlled Lincolnshire Road Car bus company.

One of the original group of streamlined A4 Pacifics, no. 2509 Silver Link, at Grantham station. ROD KNIGHT

Preserved A4 Pacific Bittern in LNER blue livery passing Moor Lane Branston 30 December 2014. GRAHAM LIGHTFOOT

THE FASTEST DUCK IN THE WORLD

On 3 July 1938 a special train was assembled on the pretext of conducting brake tests. It comprised six coaches and the all-important dynamometer car, without which no official record could have been confirmed, hauled by A4 locomotive no. 4468 Mallard. On the footplate were driver Joe Duddington, fireman Tommy Bray and inspector Sam Jenkins. Starting from the Barkston triangle, just south of Grantham, the train was slowed by a speed limit, and was only doing 24mph (40km/h) as it passed through the station.

South of the town it picked up speed, despite climbing uphill, and passed Stoke signal box, close to the tunnel, at just under 75mph (120km/h) before accelerating down Stoke Bank. Between mileposts 89 to 92, the average speed reached 120mph (192km/h) with a peak of just over 126 (205km/h) to take the record, which stands to this day. In a BBC interview later, Duddington described the experience:

I gave Mallard her head and she just jumped to it like a live thing. After three miles the speedometer in my cab showed 107mph then 108, 109, 110 and before I knew it the needle was at 116 and we'd got the record. They told me afterwards that there was a great deal of excitement in the dynamometer car. 'Go on old girl' I thought, 'she can do better than this', so I nursed her through Little Bytham at 123 and in the next 1¼ miles the needle crept up further, 123½, 124, 125 and then for a quarter of a mile while they told me the folks in the car held their breath – 126mph.

Mallard waiting at Barkston station to start its run. The dynamometer car is immediately behind the locomotive. NATIONAL RAILWAY MUSEUM/SCIENCE & SOCIETY PICTURE LIBRARY

The train had then to brake hard because of speed restrictions at Tallington, and Mallard herself had to be taken off the train at Peterborough because of an over-heated connecting rod bearing, but the deed had been done and the record established. Gresley had calculated that the train ought to have been able to reach 130mph (208km/h), and planned a second run, but World War Two stopped such frivolities.

accommodation. The train left King's Cross for Edinburgh on a Friday evening to arrive in the Scottish capital in time for a day's sightseeing. The cruise then took them to the Highlands, the Lake District and Yorkshire before coming onto the Joint Line for visits to Lincoln and Ely, returning to London by way of Cambridge. There is some doubt as to whether the land cruises actually made any money but, once again, the PR people made excellent use of the publicity they generated.

Although the exploits of the Northern Belle and *Mallard* and her sisters, well publicized by the LNER's excellent PR department, got most of the LNER attention in those years, the company was making major improvements elsewhere. It invested heavily in new goods marshalling yards, improved a large number of stations and added extra running loops and other lineside facilities, including some in Lincolnshire. One other local investment was the purchase, in 1934, of two new paddle steamers, the *Wingfield* and *Tattershall Castles*, to update the Humber ferry service.

The company was heavily involved in the 'Square Deal for the Railways' campaign – the LNER version appeared under the title of 'Fair Play for the Railways' – which was aimed at further loosening the regulatory strings that were making effective competition with road transport so difficult. 'The placing of road and rail transport on equal terms in all practical respects is essential for the proper economic use and development of the transport of the country' they claimed, but progress on the matter was halted when Britain again declared war on Germany on 3 September 1939.

For a few days nothing much changed on the LNER but, a week after the declaration, that six-hour trip to Edinburgh on the Coronation suddenly stretched to nine-and-a-half. On the same day, the passenger service on the Spilsby branch was ended 'for the duration', never to open again. The LNER's golden age had hit the wartime buffers.

Back to War – Again

On the outbreak of war, the LNER, along with the rest of the UK's railways, was put back under government control and, as in World War One, service to the general public was subordinate to the requirements of the wartime economy. In many respects, what happened was a repeat of the previous situation. Timetables were initially rewritten to provide little more than a skeleton service in the belief that heavy air attacks were imminent, but were slightly eased when the expected onslaught did not arrive. Even so, trains were slowed and diverted; buffet and restaurant cars virtually disappeared; a number of halts and minor stations were closed or had services reduced; and priority was given to goods for military purposes and passengers on official business.

Railway staff and users were all handicapped by the blackout regulations. Lighting on stations and in goods yards became almost non-existent – forty people drowned after falling into the railway docks at Grimsby or Immingham – and locomotive crews had to work under a tarpaulin canopy to prevent the glow of the fire from giving the train's position away to a night raider.

The company suffered an initial loss of personnel as staff serving in the Territorial Army were called up immediately; others volunteered later, and trained men often moved to other, better paying, wartime jobs. Such moves were banned from October 1941, with call-up of railwaymen ended

Coal from different pits on sale at Boston station in the 1930s. ROD KNIGHT

a year later, unless the company agreed that they could be released. Women filled many of the jobs made vacant. About 15,000 were taken on by the LNER, mainly into clerical and service jobs, but with many going into signalling and some into more taxing occupations. At least one track-gang on the Lincolnshire Loop was made up entirely of women, other than the male foreman, and many others may have been in existence.

The German campaigns against shipping bringing supplies to Britain began immediately this time, so Lincolnshire food production was again vitally important, as was the ability to move those goods to all parts of the country. The threat from road vehicles was reduced by fuel rationing, and the railways had to step up to the mark to keep things moving. The county's engineering works once again moved into wartime production mode. Marshall's at Gainsborough built naval guns and miniature submarines, in addition to its usual agricultural work,

and many other firms took on work that required new supplies of steel and other raw materials. Scunthorpe, with the aid of its new railway facilities, was able to increase production substantially. Surprisingly, it never came under aerial attack, thanks, according to local legend, to the heavy pall of smoke that continually hung over the town and its works.

Immingham was again a vital freight port, with landing craft and military vehicles from the United States arriving there for onward movement to troops within the UK, or for shipping on to Russia or other overseas battlefields. After the invasion of Europe, large amounts of fuel, ammunition and other supplies were taken there by train to be shipped to Antwerp after its liberation. Perhaps surprisingly, it escaped relatively unscathed by air raids, although Grimsby was hit by nearly forty attacks, which destroyed the fish market, warehouses and one of the fish docks.

Colliery and company wagons supplying a Scunthorpe steelworks – one of Lincolnshire's key rail-supplied war industries. ROD KNIGHT

Other towns in the county suffered from air raids, although most appeared to be the work of individual attackers. Louth had one such on 19 February 1941, when a single aircraft machine-gunned the station and the town and dropped two bombs on the railway premises. Fireman Bradley was killed – one of eight people in the town overall – with four railway staff injured. Services were stopped for a while because it was feared that a delayed action bomb had fallen alongside the tracks. Goods trains were then allowed to go through, as were empty passenger trains, after their occupants had been taken off and carried by bus to Ludborough, the next station south, where they could rejoin the carriages. A railway inspector decided there was no bomb, so normal service was resumed, but a bomb squad officer later contradicted that opinion, and trains were stopped again, while he dealt with the explosives.

Further down the same line, a bomb on Alford station caused the town's only fatality during the war, when it destroyed the goods shed and the adjacent yard crane.

Attack by Moonlight

Woodhall Junction was machine-gunned by a solitary night fighter – the bullets were reported to be still in the signal box woodwork when demolished forty years later. Signalman Tommy Gaunt, on duty at the time, did not like moonlit nights during the war – he believed the river stood out too clearly as a guide for German aircraft. Tommy, who had served in the Royal Engineers during World War One, hadn't wanted to be there at all – he had been a signalman at Spalding but moved to Woodhall Junction to avoid the night shifts at Spalding. Shortly after his move, they started nights at the Junction as troop trains and munitions began to move.

Skegness was also bombed in 1940 and 1941, with the station hit in the latter year, fortunately without casualties, but the town, and the other resorts suffered more from the restrictions on travel, including the 'Is Your Journey Really Necessary?' campaign. Much of the Lincolnshire coast was also closed to the public, as a military precaution. Rail arrivals for

Easter at Skegness numbered over 17,000 in 1939, but only 2,000 in 1940, although it rose to just under 5,000 by 1944. Some traffic was generated by about 80,000 army recruits arriving there for basic training and several thousand more to the Butlin's camp, now renamed HMS Royal Arthur and used as a naval training centre.

Rural Lincolnshire was an evacuation area for children from South and West Yorkshire and Hull, as well as for those being moved from Grimsby and Cleethorpes. Trainloads from Yorkshire arrived in Lincoln, Louth and other centres early in 1939, from where they were distributed to the relative safety of villages in the countryside. Oddly, those from Hull went to almost the furthest part of the county, travelling by bus to Boston, since the Humber ferries were considered not to be safe.

It wasn't just children that were moved to the Lincolnshire lines for safety, Pullman cars were kept at Stixwould station, where they were moved and heated every so often to keep them in good order.

Nationally, locomotives and rolling stock were pooled to ensure availability, which meant that surprising combinations could often be found in improbable locations. Michael Hubbard, the son of a wartime station master on the Lincolnshire Loop, remembered one of the streamlined A4 Pacifics using the line with a diverted Edinburgh service. He couldn't remember the locomotive name but claimed the train was the *Flying Scotsman*, but such names were not used during the war. The loco was 'filthy' he said, in war-time black livery. He was even more surprised by the appearance of a Southern Railway Schools' class locomotive passing through on a troop train far away from its normal area of operations.

An armoured train, manned by Polish soldiers, operated along the East Lincolnshire line, as well as on the seaside loops. It was initially based at a variety of locations, but eventually 'settled' at Boston. A tank locomotive hauled two wagons plus two armoured 'gun platforms' mounting six-pounder guns. The soldiers also carried anti-tank 'bazookas', machine guns and other weapons.

Evacuees arriving at Goxhill station in 1939. ANN BOULTON

The railways also contributed to, and occasionally suffered from, the Home Guard. Many did an excellent job of fire watching and generally keeping eyes open for unauthorized travellers in an area, but some of their activities were less approved of. One platoon tried to blow up a mined railway bridge having misunderstood a signal to mean that a German invasion was taking place. Fortunately for the trains, but worryingly for national defence, the charges failed to damage the bridge.

Bomber County Goes to War

The biggest single change between World War One and World War Two in Lincolnshire was that the county found itself very much in the military front line during World War Two. It became 'Bomber County', the base for part of the Royal Air Force's Bomber Command, Britain's main strike force against Germany and its allies during much of the war. There were also a number of training and

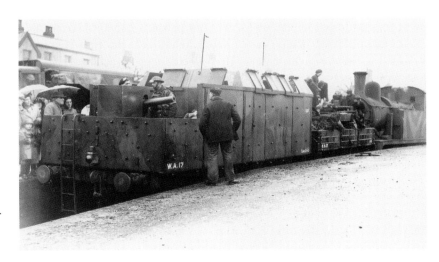

Armoured train on display to the public in Lincoln Central during a War Weapons Week in World War Two.
PETER GREY

fighter stations and an array of support and control facilities. Seventy locations, including forty-six active airfields, had to be supplied with personnel, fuel, bombs, other armaments and all the materials needed by a community of several tens of thousands of men and women. Many of those supplies came by train to a number of railheads in the county.

Personnel travelled to and from their bases by train by warrant or, occasionally, by subterfuge. The last train out of Lincoln to the station for RAF Woodhall Spa and the camps there, holding troops for the Arnhem operation, was too long to fit the station platforms, and also blocked the level-crossing serving the swing bridge over the River Witham. Servicemen who had not obtained a ticket at Lincoln would leap out onto the blacked-out platform, run round the loco and back down the far platform, then stand claiming to be crossing the river from the pub rather than having travelled there by train.

Most of Lincolnshire's aviation fuel was distributed from a single location at Torksey. It was a commercial site operated by Shell/BP, fed by rail from a refinery at Stanlow and by barge along the River Trent. From there, rail tankers could move it to locations closer to the bases where it was transferred to road vehicles.

Rationing of all fuels during the war meant that the goods being transported were in great demand. There was organized theft and black-market trading, but some 'findings' were more acceptable. One stationmaster observed that one wagon of a long train of 100 octane aviation fuel, held in a siding at his station, was leaking. He collected the leak in a bucket and saved its contents for a son with a motorcycle. On a more basic level, David Winter, a child of a level-crossing keeper, said that his mum gave all the engine drivers a cup of tea, in return for which a lump of coal would 'drop off' as the engine passed.

The other large military traffic was the bombs and other munitions being supplied to the airfields. Three maintenance units – bomb stores – were set up at RAF Norton Disney, RAF Market Stainton and RAF South Witham. Norton Disney opened

in 1939, served by the adjacent railway station at Swinderby on the old Midland branch from Newark to Lincoln, and supplied munitions, plus other dangerous supplies, including oxygen for the use of aircrews. Similar activities took place at South Witham, which was laid out in ancient woodland on the Lincolnshire–Rutland border, and Market Stainton, opening in 1943 on the Wolds in the north-east of the county. At Market Stainton up to 20,000 tons of bombs could be stored at any one time alongside about 60 miles (100km) of local roads, which were closed to the public for the purpose. The existence of a number of 'drove' roads, once used to move herds of cattle to grazing areas on the coast, meant the verges were unusually wide, making them particularly good for the purpose. Bombs were delivered to the station at Donington on Bain, which had the advantage of lying between two tunnels on the Louth-to-Bardney branch, both of which could be used to hold complete trains of munitions, although they caused a problem on one occasion when a locomotive was sent that was too large to pass through the tunnel, resulting in bombs for that night's planned raids not getting through. On another occasion, several wagons of bombs ran away on the branch; they continued for several miles before coming to rest a short distance from the junction at Bardney. Fortunately, there were no other trains on the line at the time.

Airfield building and upgrading took place constantly during the war, with much construction material arriving by rail. Aby was the railhead for the construction of RAF Strubby and Firsby goods yard dealt with similar items required by RAF East Kirkby.

Less warlike traffic was moved in May 1945 when food was loaded onto Lancaster bombers to be dropped to the people of the Netherlands. Operation Manna made use of several Lincolnshire airfields and is credited with helping avoid large-scale starvation in the Dutch towns and countryside.

A sadder operation ran from a number of stations close to the airfields. Signalman Percy Carter described how a box wagon was permanently stationed at Dogdyke holding coffins for aircrew

killed in action but not lost with an aircraft. That wagon served RAF Coningsby, another was located at Stickney for East Kirkby and there would have been the same for all the other airfields. One female member of station staff said she had complained to the stationmaster about the lack of respect being shown. She wanted some form of refrigerated vehicle to be used at the very least, but Percy felt that no sympathy could be shown. He saw as many as fourteen casualties in a night at Dogdyke, with the oldest being only 27.

Belongings were similarly disposed of – anything found in an airman's locker was bundled up and sent away because the new crews needed the space. He remembered a bike left by a crewman who disappeared, which was kept for six months, then sent to London. The owner's parents made contact two years later – their son was a prisoner of war, where was his bike?

Pride at Achievements

At the end of the war, as in the previous conflict, the railways found themselves run down, short of equipment and facilities, and still under direct

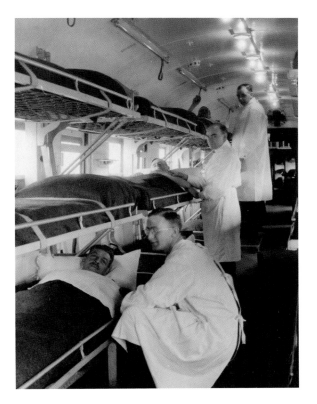

Medical staff caring for wounded soldiers on board the train. LINCS TO THE PAST, REF LCL 6041b

government control. Despite that, the LNER PR department felt the company could look back with pride on its achievements during the conflict.

> The total value of the damage sustained from all forms of enemy action was greater than that suffered by any other railway. It bore the brunt of the huge coal traffic movements that had to be made to feed the war factories and the Home Front. And whilst dealing with a greater agricultural traffic than ever before in its history, the LNER sustained the bomber offensive of the RAF and the USAF, for no less than three-quarters of all the nation's bomber airfields were located on its system. The slag, the tarmac, the cement, and the bricks that went to build those airfields and the personnel, the stores, the petrol and the bombs needed for servicing them were moved by the LNER.

Not all of the railway staff felt similarly happy. Many women were laid off as men returned to their jobs. One such may well have been being described in the March 1947 LNER magazine:

> On December 24, Mrs E. V. Beckett, signalwoman, who recently completed her term of employment, was presented with an electro-plated milk jug and sugar basin as a parting gift from the staff and friends. The presentation was made by Mr F. Fisk, stationmaster, who spoke very highly of Mrs Beckett's association with the Company. Mrs Beckett has been a signalwoman since March 1943, *she is the last woman to hold such a position in the Lincoln district*, and she is in the unique position of working in the same signal box as her husband, Mr C. Beckett, on the opposite turn.

'Forward' to the Future

The LNER board and its senior staff had other things on their minds. Post-war, the threat of nationalization was back again. The Labour Party proposed large-scale industrial takeovers in its manifesto for the 1945 General Election, including most of the national transport systems, and its victory saw legislation brought forward to take them into public ownership. The railway companies fought back, with the support, on this occasion, of the road transport lobby, who were facing the same threat. Under its motto 'Forward' the LNER announced a £50 million five-year plan that would have seen 1,000 new locomotives constructed to ten standard designs, replacing a similar number from forty-nine existing classes, along with over 5,000 coaches – despite the fact that the carriage works at both York and Doncaster had been destroyed during the war – and 70,000 wagons. More electrification was already under way with additional routes planned, track upgrades carried out and new steamships built to replace those lost on active service or by enemy action.

In Lincolnshire, the two existing passenger stations at Grimsby and the East Marsh goods yard were to be replaced by a single new complex incorporating a passenger, goods and coal facilities. Lincoln was to have better offices and a modernized locomotive depot; a large marshalling yard was planned at Spalding; new loops would be added to the Towns Line near Grantham; and the station at Cleethorpes was to be substantially upgraded.

Just how much would eventually have been affordable is uncertain, since parts depended on government compensation for losses suffered during the war, but it was a bold plan, and much of it was carried out later. One prescient project approved by the LNER, but dropped by the new owners, was the East Coast diesel scheme, which would have seen twenty-five diesel electric locomotives purchased to pull many of the main-line expresses.

The LNER did offer a last-minute alternative to outright nationalization. In 'The State and the Railways', published in October 1946, it proposed that the government should buy the track and other fixed assets of the railways, paying for them in interest-bearing government stocks. These would then be leased back to the companies on a long-term basis, who would maintain and operate the railways for the period of that lease. The scheme

The post-war – all-male – track gang at Goxhill. ANN BOULTON

would, they said, achieve 'the finest possible service to the travelling public and the trader, regular employment for the staff at a fair level of wages and under the best possible conditions, and for the stockholders a fair and reasonable return on their investment'.

The idea was not backed by the other railway companies or by the government – the Minister of Transport reportedly 'dismissed it with a single sentence' – although something very similar was to come into place many years later. Under the Transport Act of 1947, the future of the railways was to be taken out of the hands of the LNER and its counterparts elsewhere in the country. The terms, according to the LNER's Sir Ronald Matthews, would have brought 'a blush of shame to the leathery cheek of a Barbary pirate', but the government paid just under a billion pounds for what the Chancellor of the Exchequer described as 'a very poor bag of assets', which were 'a disgrace to the country'. Public ownership came in on 1 January 1948 and the future was now in the hands of the Railway Executive Board of the British Transport Commission, although many of its decisions were to be taken by railwaymen who moved from the companies into the new structure.

New facilities in Lincoln station refreshment rooms. ROD KNIGHT

CHAPTER 9

Optimism and Modernization

Under the 1947 Transport Act, the British Transport Commission (BTC) took control of the railways, as well as road goods transport, canals, docks, London Transport and a variety of other businesses that had been owned by the railways. These included hotels, steamer services, police forces, the Pickford's haulage business and the travel agents, Thomas Cook, which had been taken over jointly by the big four railways companies during World War Two. The Commission also acquired a number of road passenger services, as well as the non-controlling interests in bus and coach companies that had been held by the railways.

The railways themselves were operated as British Railways, by the Railway Executive, one of five such bodies set up by the BTC under 'schemes of delegation'. The Executive in turn devolved many of its powers to six regions, with Lincolnshire once again in a single unit – the Eastern Region, other than the remaining LMSR interests, which came under the control of the Midland, although they were transferred to the Eastern in the 1950s. George Houlden, still portering in Lincolnshire, again felt that little changed at operational levels, but some other ex-railwaymen did feel a sense of pride in their 'ownership' of the system. One agreed

Class O2 2–8–0 no. 63960 carrying the original BRITISH RAILWAYS on the tender climbing past the power station at Lincoln Stamp End heading towards Grimsby in 1950. PETER GREY

Britannia Class Standard Pacific 70040 Clive of India *at Spalding station in June 1961.* JACK RAY

that 'the bosses were still there' but argued that the presence of trade unionist 'Bill' Allen, previously General Secretary of the Association of Locomotive Engineers and Firemen, on the Board of the Executive, and responsible for staff matters, gave him a greater feeling of 'being looked after'. Others, including Mr Allen's ex-colleagues at ASLEF, and the other unions, were less convinced when rail pay failed to keep up with rising rates in the improving post-war economy.

The early years of British Railways saw a continuation of the progress made by the companies in repairing war-time damage and catching up on long-delayed maintenance projects. There were some sensible moves, such as the decision to standardize new steam locomotive building to less than a dozen types, rather than the 400 or so then at work on the lines, although the logic rather went out of the window as many locos were still built to old designs as well as to the new ones. The decision to continue with steam has been heavily criticized, but the argument was that coal was easily available

locally, whereas oil for diesels had to be imported and electrification would be expensive and take much longer. Similar plans were introduced for coaching stock, and the new organization kept control of all the privately owned goods wagons that had been expropriated during the war, although large numbers of dilapidated ones were rapidly scrapped in favour of more modern equipment.

The ongoing need for goods to help rebuild the national economy saw traffic on Lincolnshire's main lines continue in a healthy state; the experience of a terrible harvest in 1947 saw the rural lines continue to be key to food transport and a return to the seaside by the holidaymakers and day trippers all gave an appearance of good health to the county's railways. Grantham even saw the return of named

The largest of the BR Standard steam classes, 9F goods no. 92193 passes Holme Street Crossing in Grimsby. April 1961. JOHN FOREMAN

Some stations would have contributed little to railway income. Eastoft (ABOVE) on the AJR was still technically open in 1960 and Five Mile House (BELOW)(BRIAN ROSE), on the Lincolnshire Loop was said to be so called because that was the distance to the nearest habitation!

levels of receipts during the summer season, but were poorly used at other times. The third included most of the rural branches and the Loop, which survived on a meagre diet of local goods traffic and some passenger receipts, where those services had survived.

Personal service on such lines could be good, but often wildly uneconomic. One lady from Kirkstead went for a day's hunting in the winter of 1948–49 for a meet at Hainton. Her two horses were put into a horsebox that had been brought to Woodhall Junction and there attached to a train. They were taken off at Bardney and attached to the Louth train as far as South Willingham. The horsebox remained in the station there while they hunted, then returned the same way. The cost was £2 for two horses and their riders.

Some lines continued to carry useful levels of goods. Peter Wakefield, who lived at Billingborough station while his father was stationmaster there in the 1950s, described how goods trains could leave there for Sleaford with sixty loaded wagons, the maximum allowed behind 'a valiant J6'. He remembered the 'great excitement' of a farmer moving his equipment, lock, stock and barrel, to Norfolk, and how the local mattress company would send a van-load of feathers to London – a 12-ton van would carry a ton of feathers!

Road Competition Returns

A major blow to the railway system was the political decision by the new Conservative administration, elected in 1951, to denationalize road transport. The BTC had attempted to build an integrated road and rail system, with the state-owned British Road Services (BRS) carrying much local trade, but the Transport Act of 1953 saw a large number of BRS vehicles sold to private owners who were able to compete strongly for local and long-distance traffic. In Lincolnshire, this change was felt most in the agricultural sector, where large numbers of movements were relatively short haul, and rail carriage might require one or more changes of transport mode between source and destination.

trains, although it only caught a glimpse of one, the Capitals Limited, later the Elizabethan, since it ran non-stop London to Edinburgh. However, such impressions hid a deeper malaise. In reality, Lincolnshire's lines could be divided into three rough categories. The first was the lines that maintained a healthy level of goods and passenger traffic, such as the Towns Line; the ex-GCR lines serving Scunthorpe, Immingham and Grimsby; the Joint Line from Gainsborough to Spalding and possibly the East Lincolnshire and the Grimsby–Lincoln–Grantham route to London. The second included the seaside services; the M&GNR; Grantham to Boston and the New Line, which showed good

SNOW ON THE LINES

The early months of 1947 saw very heavy snowfalls, which caused difficulty across the rail network. In Lincolnshire, the lines through the Wolds were badly affected, with Grimsby cut off for a period, with both the East Lincolnshire Line and the old Great Central routes blocked by drifts. Railwayman Percy Carter, sent out with a pole to determine the depths of the snow, claimed to have hit one object while poking down only to find it was the top of a telegraph pole. A fish train got stuck in a drift near Louth, blocking the line and causing passengers on other trains to have to spend a night in Louth, North Thoresby or Ludborough. The Grimsby Town football team, on its way home from a match, was among the stranded travellers. The line to New Holland was also blocked, but the Hull ferries were diverted into Grimsby instead. Coal and milk were short, as were potatoes, although that was mainly because the supplies were frozen into the earthen storage clamps in the countryside.

The Royal Air Force tried to be of assistance, deploying a pair of their new jet engines, mounted on a railway wagon, to try to blast the show clear. The technique was effective, in fact too effective, since the jet exhaust blew away ballast and set fire to the sleepers. It then blew itself off the line when it met a particularly stubborn blockage near Ludborough.

When the thaw came, the county's railways met new difficulties as floods of meltwater affected Spalding, Boston and Gainsborough, where the Trent burst its banks.

Inspector R. Fry (far right) and colleagues in the snow at Navenby in 1947. FRY FAMILY

Gyron Junior jet engines mounted on a rail wagon for snow clearing duties.

The changes also affected the transport of fish from Grimsby. Writing in 1958 about a visit to the town, G. Freeman Allen noted that, although eight express fish trains left the port every day, with the trade supplemented by individual wagons attached to passenger trains, many merchants were switching to road transport. Large wholesalers had built up their own fleets, and many others were moving their larger consignments by road with 'uneconomic consignments of the odd box or two' being left to the railways. He reported that Sir Reginald Wilson, Chairman of the Eastern Area Board, had declared Grimsby Docks to be 'a grave financial liability' and threatened to withdraw poorly supported services. The 'fast fish' trains, hauled by

Some traffic was not easily transferred to the road. A large casting shipped into Grimsby for delivery to Scunthorpe. NORTH EAST LINCOLNSHIRE COUNCIL LIBRARY SERVICE, LOCAL HISTORY COLLECTION

Britannia no. 70038 Robin Hood *leaving Grimsby with a fast fish train on its way to London.* JACK RAY

express locomotives such as the new Britannia Class Pacifics – to the delight of 'spotters' on the East Lincolnshire Line – would continue to run for a few years, but their viability was declining.

A report in the 1951 *Railway Magazine* described a rail tour of Lincolnshire conducted by three friends the previous year. They paid 17/6d (87p) each for a week's Holiday Runabout ticket and travelled about 1,400 miles (2,300km). They reported that the trains were clean and punctual, but that slow, 'inefficient' station staff caused delays, although these could often be made up by friendly and enthusiastic drivers. One trip, from Lincoln to Mablethorpe, was already twelve minutes late when it left the second stop, at Five Mile House, but the elderly class J11 'Pom-Pom' made up the lost time by Firsby.

Such feats were soon to be consigned to the history books, since an unusual sight was seen on Lincolnshire lines in 1952, when an ex-GWR diesel railcar was tested on a number of services. The trial was deemed to be a success and the county was chosen for a larger-scale introduction of new units being built by British Railways' workshops. Thirteen sets would do the job, comprising ten to cover Cleethorpes to Lincoln, and Grimsby to Skegness, Barton and New Holland, and the Louth-to-Willoughby Loop, with three spares. The proposal was resisted by the British Transport Commission, who, ironically, were concerned about the effects on the bus services operated by the Commission-owned Lincolnshire Road Car. Their objections were withdrawn and a third of a million pounds was paid for the units, which were ordered from Derby works in late 1953. The first went into service in January 1955 and proved popular and efficient, with more passengers carried on more frequent, faster and cleaner trains.

Although the new diesels made the local passenger services much more viable, there were still many stations and lines where losses were being made. The 1950s were a very good time for Lincolnshire's coastal resorts, but the railways'

GWR diesel railcar on trial in Lincolnshire. 1952. THE FAMILY OF INSPECTOR FRY *(on extreme right)*

Diesel multiple units (DMUs) at Willoughby station in 1964. The nearer unit is travelling from Grimsby to Peterborough, the further one serves the branch to Mablethorpe. P.C. LOFTIS

The ex-Great Central locomotive depot in Lincoln was taken over to house the new DMUs. ROD KNIGHT

LINCOLN RAIL ACCIDENTS

Lincoln suffered two significant accidents in the post-war years. The first took place in October 1949 when a nearly new Pacific no. 60123, later named *H. A. Ivatt* after a GNR locomotive engineer, derailed with a goods train on the Lincoln Avoiding Line and had to be retrieved by crane from the bottom of one of the embankments. Fortunately, no one was hurt in the incident, and the locomotive was restored to service, although a number of wagons were badly damaged.

That was not the case for the second event, which took place on 3 June 1962 and involved a sleeping-car train from King's Cross to Edinburgh, diverted through Lincoln due to engineering work on the ECML. The driver in charge of the train did not know the route, and the

locomotive was being driven by an experienced steam driver with little experience of diesel traction. The train took a 15mph (24km/h) curve on the approach to the station at what was estimated to have been nearly four times the permitted speed. Most of the coaches left the rails, although the locomotive, a new English Electric Type 4 – later class 40 – remained upright. Two passengers and a sleeping-car attendant were killed and seven others injured. The inspector investigating the accident said the driver had 'grossly underestimated the speed at which the train was travelling, largely due to his inexperience of diesels'. He laid part of the blame on the original driver for permitting the less-experienced man to take charge of the train.

Pacific 60123 partly buried under wagon wreckage after its derailment. R. FRY

Derailed sleeping cars after the crash of June 1962. PETER GREY

Ex-LMS 5F 2–6–0 no. 42823 takes an excursion home to the Midlands from Skegness past a fine array of GN somersault signals at Firsby South Junction. ROD KNIGHT

share of the business was shrinking steadily, with only a third of travellers to Skegness arriving by rail by the middle of the decade.

The resorts were also hit by the East Coast floods of early 1952, when the sea defences at Mablethorpe, Sutton-on-Sea and other locations were destroyed by high tides and a storm surge. Once back in operation, the railways took a significant role in the movement of materials for the repairs, with slag, a by-product of the iron and steel working at Scunthorpe, proving to be a valuable commodity in filling the gaps.

Cravens Class 105 DMU at Mablethorpe station ready to leave for the East Lincs at Willoughby. JACK RAY

Sutton-on-Sea in the aftermath of the 1953 floods. The LNER sign was still in place six years after the company ceased to exist. D.N. ROBINSON

Modernization, but at a Cost

Inevitably, closures were in the air, especially after the arrival of the Modernization and Re-Equipment Plan of December 1954. This proposed a rapid changeover to diesel and electric traction on the main lines, as well as the rural services, better track and signalling, a concentration of goods into a smaller number of larger facilities, and general improvements to the system. The cost was to be £1,200 million – a greater sum than the original purchase price of the railways – but the plan was expected to provide the country with a 'fully efficient and economic' railway system, 'adaptable to meet the requirements for many years to come'.

Improvements were made in Lincolnshire, with goods facilities upgraded, as well as the better passenger trains. A new goods shed was built in Lincoln, four times the size of the one it replaced, designed, according to the *Lincolnshire Echo*, 'to deal with 260 tons of railway traffic daily, consisting of many thousands of individual packages, and all the work would be done in one shift'. The building cost £200,000, and was officially opened on 16 January 1959.

The new shed was described as 'of the largest single-span buildings in the country', although, ironically, British Railways was doing away with another covered space in the city at about the same time, when it removed the overall roof from St Mark's station.

The goods facilities in the north of the county were also improved by a reorganization of sidings and a new marshalling yard at Scunthorpe.

Scunthorpe West was a hump yard for the gravity sorting of wagons, and was the only one of its type in the county. Goods services were also being concentrated at the larger centres and distribution points, with important yards at Grimsby, Barnetby,

Scunthorpe West new yard. SCUNTHORPE TELEGRAPH

Boston and Grantham, in addition to Lincoln and Scunthorpe.

Closures of lines or services had, of course, been going on for many years, but they accelerated in the 1950s. The first to suffer complete closure was Bourne–Essendine, in 1951, despite strong protests being lodged by Bourne Council and others.

64241 calls at Halton Holegate on the Spilsby branch on 22 November 1956, two years before closure of the line. STEVE PRIESTLEY

LAST TRAIN TO ESSENDINE

The *Stamford Mercury* reported the final Bourne and Essendine round trip on Saturday 16 June under the heading: 'Janet's Last Trip on Bourne Line'.

It described the scene just before 8pm as *Janet*, 2–6–0 tender loco no. 43062, was getting ready to leave Bourne station for the final round trip on the line. The scene was 'one of extreme gaiety' despite the flying of a black flag of mourning alongside a Union flag, flown at half-mast on the engine itself. The occasion was 'more like an opening than a closure' as the train received a 'hearty send-off with similar scenes of noisy, excited children and bangs and smoke from exploding fog detonators as it departed.

Crowds had gathered at the intermediate stations at Thurlby and Braceborough Spa, with additional passengers joining the train until, for the first time in many years, and possibly ever, there was standing room only as it steamed into Essendine. After trains from Peterborough and Grantham had made their connections, there was even less room, but 'at precisely 8.51pm', it left Essendine to the accompaniment of more detonator explosions, which continued to the Carlby Bridge.

The festivities were the classic model for closures, but so were the comments of travellers. The paper reported that the final passengers were 'in a quieter and sadder mood as they handed their tickets to station master Mr A. C. Scott', but for many of them it may well have been their first trip, as well as their last.

Research had shown that the average number of passengers carried by each train was five, and the only significant goods traffic, apart from coal, was sugar beet and potatoes, shipped out in the winter months.

'Let Them Walk Home'

Five months later, in October, goods services were withdrawn from the portion of the North Lindsey beyond West Halton, passenger traffic having ceased many years earlier. Passenger trains ceased on the Louth-to-Bardney Line the following month, and to Horncastle in November 1954. The driver of the last service to Horncastle commented that he wanted to stop the train half-way and leave the passengers to walk home, in view of their previous lack of support for the railway.

Closures then came piecemeal, sometimes of lines, sometimes of stations and often of either goods or passenger traffic. Barkston, on the ECML, and Helpringham, Nocton and Dunston and Potterhanworth, on the Joint Line, all closed in 1955, with Old Leake, on the East Lincolnshire Line going the following year. Skellingthorpe station, the only Lincolnshire stop on the LD&ECR, left the county railway map in 1955 when passenger trains ceased to run on the line, although goods continued for another quarter century. The Epworth-to-Haxey portion of the Axholme Joint closed in February 1956. Goods on the eastern end of the Louth-to-Bardney Line ended in September 1956, with the line gradually cut back over the next four years with the final stretch, from Bardney to Wragby, closing in February 1960. The old GNR station in Stamford, Stamford East, closed in March 1957, with the traffic diverted into Stamford Town, although passenger services only survived for a further two years. The same meeting that agreed the closure of Stamford East also called time on the rest of Lincolnshire's stations on the ECML, with the sole exception of Grantham. Essendine itself was one; the others were Tallington, Little Bytham and Corby Glen. Spilsby to Firsby, closed to passen-

The last passenger train from Louth to Bardney on 3 November 1951. The driver was W. Cartwright (holding lamp on right), the fireman F. Hardy (left of lamp). MALCOLM WHITE

The last train on the Axholme Joint – a special chartered by Crowle school in April 1965. SCUNTHORPE TELEGRAPH

gers 'for the duration of the war', went completely in November 1958.

The End of the M&GNR

The biggest shock of the 1950s came in 1958, with the closure of most of the M&GNR. The BTC had established a Branch Lines Committee in 1949 with a brief to close the least-used branch lines, and the Eastern Region had set up another body in 1958 to consider the future of the M&GNR. It recommended shutting down much of the system. Among the factors were: significant duplication of lines, particularly at the Norfolk end; a very seasonal passenger traffic based on summer visits to the Norfolk coast; a rapidly declining agricultural trade; and the supposed high cost of rebuilding the bridge over the Nene at King's Lynn. It was estimated that a million pounds a year could be saved in addition to an immediate £500,000 that would not have to be spent on engineering work.

Under the initial proposals, all the passenger services on the Lincolnshire lines would go, as would through-goods traffic, although Spalding to Sutton Bridge would still carry local produce. On 11 November, the East Midlands Consultative Committee, meeting in Bourne, approved the plans for the county, with the only change being the retention of Spalding to Bourne and on to Billingborough for goods. From Bourne as far west as South

Witham, the lines would be closed and lifted. The final day of through-services was 28 February 1959.

Closures of lines and stations around the county continued through the early 1960s. The Leverton branch from Retford to Lincoln closed in November 1959, although the section to Cottam power station in Nottinghamshire reopened in 1968 to carry coal, and the Lincolnshire end served an oil depot on the Trent at Torksey from 1966 to 1988. The Louth-to-Mablethorpe part of the Louth-to-Willoughby Loop closed in December 1960, although Mablethorpe itself remained open. Most of the smaller stations on the East Lincolnshire Line lost their passenger trains in 1961, with goods following three years later. The same fate befell all remaining stations on the Joint Line other than Spalding, Sleaford, Lincoln and Gainsborough, and on the southern section of the Loop. The Grimsby to Immingham Electric Railway had been cut back at the Grimsby end in 1956, but the whole line closed in July 1961, despite still carrying large numbers of passengers. The Consultative Committee noted the high usage, but was persuaded that staffing costs were too high because of the large number of single-unit trams required and that much capital investment would be needed if the line was to remain open.

Stopping passenger trains were withdrawn in 1962 from all the stations on the Lincoln-to-Honington Line other than Leadenham, and Harmston closed completely. All trains were

The last trip on the Grimsby to Immingham Electric Railway. NORTH EAST LINCOLNSHIRE COUNCIL LIBRARY SERVICE, LOCAL HISTORY COLLECTION

Closed stations were soon targets for vandals, especially when, like Mumby Road, they were some distance from the villages they served. P.C. LOFTIS

withdrawn in 1963 from the section of the Lincolnshire Loop between Coningsby Junction and Boston, with Tattershall, Dogdyke and Langrick stations closing. Longer distance loco-hauled services on the Cleethorpes-to-Leeds route by way of Doncaster were reduced in 1964.

Although all these changes met with local resistance, none succeeded in reversing the decisions, but, as it turned out, they were minor inconveniences compared to the hurricane that was about to hit Lincolnshire's railways. Dr Richard Beeching released his report 'The Reshaping of British Railways' on 27 March 1963.

The Beeching Cuts

The report identified 2,363 stations and 5,000 miles (8,000km) of railway line that ought to be closed in order to try to reduce the losses being experienced by the railway system. This represented just over half of the stations in the UK and nearly a third of the track mileage.

In Lincolnshire, the proposals involved what has been described as 'wholesale slaughter' of the county's services, particularly those in the east and south. The surveys of passenger and goods traffic showed that the county was not making

good use of its network. Only two sections of line – Lincoln to Newark and the Grimsby to the Ulceby triangle – achieved a loading of between 10,000 and 50,000 passengers per week, with three more – Barnetby to New Holland, Grimsby to Peterborough and Lincoln to Gainsborough – achieving between 5,000 and 10,000. Every other line carried fewer than 5,000, in many cases a lot fewer. In goods terms we did rather better, with Ulceby to Scunthorpe, most of the Joint Line and the old LD&ECR carrying over 100,000 tons. The tonnage on a number of lines was boosted by the transport of iron ore from the mines in the Grantham area, which took a variety of rather circuitous routes to Scunthorpe in order to avoid the busy East Coast Main Line.

The report recommended the removal of passenger services from the lines to the Humber ferries; the old East Lincolnshire Line; the Lincolnshire Loop between Lincoln, Boston, Spalding and Peterborough; all the coastal resorts other than Cleethorpes; and the Lincoln-to-Newark Line. In most cases, the lines themselves would be lost, although parts were to remain open as goods or through-routes. Lincoln to Grantham was to be retained as a diversionary route for ECML trains when that line had to be closed for work on the tracks. Passenger services between Lincoln and

Iron ore trains from the Grantham area had to be reversed at Barnetby after travelling by way of Lincoln. Type 1 diesel shunts the train while a class 114 DMU waits in a siding. August 1970.
KEN FISHER

Grimsby/Cleethorpes and those from Grantham to Boston were to be 'modified', although his 1965 follow-up report 'The Development of the Major Railway Trunk Routes' identified Newark–Lincoln–Grimsby and Grimsby–Doncaster as having potential for development, following a decision to reprieve Lincoln–Newark and to close Lincoln–Honington instead. A new link between the Lincoln–Nottingham Line and the East Coast Main Line was installed at Newark in 1965 to allow trains from St Mark's station to access the trunk route, and some goods services were transferred

from the East Lincolnshire line to join the ECML there rather than at Peterborough.

Following the publication of the report, a group of local authorities and other interested parties set up the Lincolnshire Railway Protection Association to campaign against the closure of the East Lincolnshire Line and its branches, but the government rejected their arguments and accepted the principles of the report. Closures accelerated again despite the election of a Labour Government in 1964. Its leader, Harold Wilson, who became Prime Minister, had promised to 'halt the main programme of rail closures ... pending a national transport survey'. Closures were certainly not halted in Lincolnshire. All goods services at stations between Lincoln and Grantham ended in 1964, as did those between Willoughby and Mablethorpe. In July of that year, traffic ended on most of the NLLR, apart from the newer line to Flixborough by way of Roxby. Goods trains between Spalding, Bourne, Billingborough and Sutton Bridge, and on remaining sections of the Axholme Joint, ran for the last time in the spring of 1965. In all those cases this represented the closure of the lines concerned, although some remained *in situ* for a time afterwards. The Lincoln-to-Honington Line, which had lost its *raison d'être*, following the change in policy referred to above, was reduced to a small stub known as the Bracebridge Branch, serving Lincoln gasworks from Lincoln itself, until December 1970. The same inquiry into that line also considered the

Woodhall Junction on 13 July 1969, a year before closure. MARY COOK

future of eight stations on the Lincoln-to-Barnetby Line. All closed on the same day as the Honington Line, leaving only Market Rasen to serve the local public.

The lines from Grimsby to Gainsborough and to Doncaster remained in use, although intermediate stations again lost either or both of their goods and passenger trains. On the Doncaster route, Medge

Hall went in 1960 and Appleby and Barnby Dun in 1967, while the original MS&LR line through Gainsborough saw Northorpe close in 1955, Blyton in 1959 and Scawby and Hibalstow in 1968. Closure of so many smaller stations did allow train services between the larger settlements to be faster. Some passenger trains on the Gainsborough route were transferred in 1968 to that through Scunthorpe, offering better services to the larger populations concerned.

Two public inquiries were held into the planned closures in the east of the county, and had some effect in reducing the cuts, but the biggest single series of closures in the county took place on 5 October 1970. The East Lincolnshire, the loop between Lincoln and Woodhall Junction, the New Line from there to Firsby, the Willoughby-to-Mablethorpe route and the portion of the loop between Boston and Peterborough, all closed to passengers, with most closing completely.

Agricultural traffic remained important on many Lincolnshire lines well into the 1960s. A train-load of Massey-Ferguson balers being delivered to Brigg in 1968 for local dealers Peacock and Binnington. P&B

A south-bound goods train headed by class 9F no. 92036 passes through Boston. The through tracks it is travelling on were lifted in 1975 after the ELR closed, but the outer, platform, lines remained to serve Skegness. 22 September 1958. JOHN FOREMAN

Sentenced, but Not Executed

Some of the appeals against closure had succeeded. The line to the Humber ferries remained open, although the route from Barton to Immingham lost its passenger service in October 1969 and was largely lifted by 1971. The intermediate stations had already been closed in 1963. Grimsby to Louth was kept open for goods, largely to serve the large maltings in the town. Boston to Skegness was also reprieved, after the holiday trade successfully

Class 114 DMU waits at New Holland Pier in March 1978 for passengers arriving off the Humber Ferry. JOHN FORD

A LONELY TRIP TO HORNCASTLE

A goods service, mostly of fuel to an agricultural merchant in the town, continued from Lincoln to Horncastle by way of Woodhall Junction for several months after other services ended on the route. A diesel shunting locomotive brought the train through, with the guard having to open and close all the level-crossings along the way.

One driver later reported that he forgot about the guard after passing through the final crossing and arrived in Horncastle to see an angry and out-of-breath colleague pursuing him along the permanent way. The service finally ended in April 1971, but not until after the local representative of the National Farmers' Union had persuaded British Rail to allow him to travel from Horncastle to Woodhall Junction, and to issue the final ticket for the lost trains in the area.

A class 08 shunter takes a short train of agricultural fuel tankers over the Woodhall Spa level crossing in February 1970. D.S. CROMARTY

NFU Lincolnshire County Secretary Mr Newton Loynes getting off the goods train at Woodhall Junction. R. LOYNES

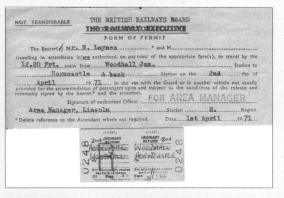

Mr Loynes' ticket, the last to be issued from Horncastle to Woodhall Junction. R. LOYNES

ABOVE: *The changing scene on one day in the early 1960s at Lincoln Central as diesel took over from steam on the main line. The train hauled by no. 70036* Boadicea *has been tentatively identified as what was known as the North Country Continental or, locally, the Boat Train, while no. D6705 is carrying the diesel head code for a Liverpool–Harwich service.*

The water crane and tank on Sleaford station being removed once locomotives no longer needed its services. LINCS TO THE PAST, REF LCL 7576

argued that the roads to the resort were so bad that a rail service was essential. Similar claims on behalf of Mablethorpe and Sutton-on-Sea failed, despite road conditions that were, and still are, worse than those to Skegness!

The section of the loop between Spalding and Peterborough had been retained as a goods and/or diversion line from the ECML, but was closed to passenger services with most the rest of the Loop Line/East Lincolnshire complex. However, a vigorous local campaign saw the service restored in June 1971, although the intermediate stations had closed earlier and were not reopened.

The End of Steam

That little diesel travelling to Horncastle was also symptomatic of another change that had been happening alongside the closure disputes. Steam traction had gone from the county by the middle 1960s, as more powerful diesel locomotives joined their diesel multiple unit (DMU) cousins on the tracks. Most commentators would agree that the transition, having been delayed much longer than on most comparable railway systems, was eventually rushed through. New diesels – Lincolnshire never seemed likely to get significant electric haulage – were ordered in large numbers without a proper testing procedure and modern steam locomotives were scrapped after just a few years' service. The change did, however, allow a great deal of the steam era infrastructure, such as coaling facilities and water cranes, to be done away with rather than maintaining two systems side by side.

New and improved rolling stock had also begun to appear on the county's lines, although many older carriages continued in use. The Horncastle

Veterans in service on the Horncastle branch in 1953. A 1901-built J11 locomotive still carrying its LNER lettering and number 4286, with an articulated pair of coaches, created in 1927 from two 1906 GNR railmotors.

and Bourne-to-Essendine services were maintained almost to the end by the pairs of ex-Great Northern steam railcars referred to earlier, and coaches designed by Sir Nigel Gresley, before he moved to the locomotive side in 1923, were to continue in service for many years yet.

On the goods side, although older, open wagons remained in service in large numbers, there was a move to a greater use of box vans, which offered better protection to the goods being carried, both from the weather and from pilfering, and there was an increasing use of specialized types. Larger and more sophisticated wagons moved coal and ore around the country, although one familiar vehicle, the white or blue 'Insulfish' van, lost its purpose when fish trains stopped running in the 1966.

The Beeching Report, and its subsequent execution, is often blamed for the meagre level of railway services in the county, but there is no doubt that he accelerated a process that was already in hand. Many lines and stations had already closed, or lost significant parts of their function, and it looked likely that that would continue. Where it is now seen as an error is in the assumption that people would be willing to drive, or take their goods, to the nearest railhead for onward transmission by rail. What actually happened was that once they were in their car, van or lorry, it was usually simpler to complete the journey by that mode of transport.

The Paytrain services, where tickets were issued while travelling, with consequent savings in station staff, made a big difference, but came into Lincolnshire in the late 1960s, too late to be taken into consideration.

Was Beeching Wrong?

Nationally, there is little doubt that Beeching was wrong to assume that goods traffic was the main function of the railways; for not having the foresight to see that new industrial and settlement patterns would require services that could make better use of currently under-used lines; and for not taking into account the expansion of motor traffic and the increased congestion it would cause, particularly in urban areas. Mathew Engel, in *Eleven Minutes Late*, felt that his biggest mistake was in not considering the role that fast, efficient long-distance passenger railways could play in the future. Sadly, even if he had, most such arguments would have cut little ice in rural, low-population Lincolnshire, although they might have stopped two major errors in later years.

Dr Beeching and his colleagues may justifiably be accused of having wielded a sledgehammer rather than a scalpel, but it was always likely that the railways of Lincolnshire would go into the last quarter of the twentieth century in a smaller state than they were in the first.

CHAPTER 10

Fading Twilight or a New Dawn?

The combined effect of the Modernization Plan and the Beeching Report was supposed to result in a modern, invigorated railway. Passengers were to be carried swiftly between major centres in diesel-powered or -hauled trains while goods would be transported in 'liner trains' – block units of container-carrying wagons that would run between major centres. Coal and minerals would travel in dedicated bulk freight and permanently coupled block trains, with even that staple of every station since the invention of the railways – coal – now carried in bulk to coal concentration stations for distribution, largely by road.

Lincolnshire saw some parts of that new world order. Grantham, as usual, did well out of the new regime. The chime whistles of Gresley's A4s were no longer heard in the town, but they had been replaced by the full-throated roar of the 3,300bhp Deltic locomotives, which took over from them on the crack services. The noise, and the concept of a loco built round an engine designed for a motor torpedo boat, gave it rather more glamour than attached to most of the early diesels. They in turn were replaced by the InterCity 125s, or High Speed Trains, almost certainly one of the best railway designs in the world at the time. Longer-distance

A4 Dwight D Eisenhower takes the last steam-hauled Glasgow–King's Cross express past Barkston Junction. 15 June 1963. JOHN FOREMAN

Class 31 D5574 and another of the same class bring an iron ore train past the Lincoln coal concentration yard in April 1969. JOHN FORD

and excursion trains still remained loco-hauled for many years, but, over much of the county, the diesel multiple unit (DMU) reigned supreme.

On the goods side, Lincolnshire continued to see large amounts of freight carried in the north of the county, with Immingham developing into one of Britain's most important docks. Coal, iron ore and steel moved to and from Scunthorpe, with oil and other products from the Humber refineries being distributed around the country. The Joint Line was still an important thoroughfare for coal and

InterCity 125 – an HST High Speed Train – near Grantham on 30 May 1978. DAVID FORD

CHANGING TRAINS ON THE AVOIDING LINE

Diverted InterCity 125 using the Avoiding Line over the River Witham in Lincoln. PETER GREY COLLECTION. COURTESY OF LINCOLNSHIRE ARCHIVES

The Durham Ox crossing at Pelham Street, with the new bridge being constructed on the left. ROD KNIGHT

The Lincoln Avoiding Line, sometimes called the High Line because it ran round the city on embankments and bridges, was part of the GN/GE Joint. Ray Heppenstall watched the trains as they passed, first as a schoolboy and an apprentice in the 1950s, then again to the end of steam in the middle 1960s.

He recalled that the majority of the trains heading east were coal to March and onwards to the south-east, and coal empties heading west. Other types of freights passed through, but no regular passenger trains, although some were occasionally seen on excursions or when services were diverted from the ECML.

The coal trains were usually pulled by WD – War Department – 2–8–0s, or other classes of the same wheel arrangement, with a variety of other types handling the lighter loads. He and his 'spotter' friends regretted the absence of 'namer' locomotives, although they did see the streamlined *East Anglia* on one occasion – possibly making them among the last people to see it in that condition, since it was going to Doncaster to have the streamlining removed.

An unusual exception to the absence of passenger trains was seen on 27 June 1958, when the royal train, hauled by two locomotives 'bulled up and with white

painted cab roofs' brought Her Majesty the Queen to open the new bridge that replaced one of Lincoln's troublesome level-crossings, that at Pelham Street.

Ray saw his first main-line diesel in June 1958, with sightings becoming more frequent through the last years of the decade, although he commented that there were 'still plenty of steam hauled workings'. Many of the diesels he saw in those years were on acceptance trials before being put into full service.

He noted his last steam working to be one of BR's 9F 2–10–0 goods engines heading a freight to March on 25 February 1965, although his last sighting of a steam locomotive on the line was an LMS design 8F waiting to move 'light engine' – with no train attached – into the goods yards on 4 March 1965.

other commodities between the north and south, although the passenger service diminished sharply. Lincoln, Grantham, Grimsby and Boston retained goods services for some years, and Stamford coal yard was still in operation until 1983.

Iron ore from the Grantham area mines continued to be carried to Scunthorpe until 1975, when the completion of the Anchor Project at the steelworks there meant that all ore would be imported from that stage on. The area then became the location for a preservation project, but we will return to that later.

Government Steps In with Social Aid

In 1968, the then Transport Minister, Barbara Castle, accepted that there might be social reasons for maintaining services, and £100,000 was provided for Cleethorpes to Newark, but it was too late for most of Lincolnshire's other threatened lines. Financial backing for the Spalding-to-Peterborough service was initially provided by the County and District Councils, who hoped that government support would be forthcoming in the future. They contributed £23,000 between them but, on being asked for a further £7,000 a year by BR, they withdrew that support from December 1975.

Meeting in Spalding the same year, the Railway Invigoration Society (RIS), later the Railway Development Society, backed the Spalding campaign and called for improved overall rail facilities in the county, and for new or reopened stations at Peakirk, Deeping St Nicholas, Donington and Helpringham.

They did have some success. Services were improved on the Sleaford-to-Doncaster route, with a new station opened on a trial basis at Ruskington in May 1975, followed by a similar experiment at Metheringham later the same year; both are still in operation. But suggestions that Donington, Gosberton and Sibsey should be added were not taken up. In a letter to the RIS, the County Planning Officer commented that, although 'serious consideration' had been given to further reopenings, the council wanted to have time to evaluate the initial experiments. Restoring passenger services to goods-only lines would be too expensive, and extending the Peterborough–Spalding trains on to Boston would not be possible, since the trackbed was to be taken over as the new route of the A16 road between the towns.

Despite these minor successes, Lincolnshire's once comprehensive, if inefficient, railway network was now a shrunken remnant of its previous self. Even where lines had been kept, stations had gone – out of the 190 or so stations at the peak of its coverage in the 1900s, only 42 remained by 1971, with Ruskington and Metheringham making it 44 in 1975.

Local Goods Depart

Private sidings for goods other than in the industrial or port complexes of Scunthorpe, Grimsby and Immingham closed down all over the county as charges for connections rose and traffic diminished. Boston docks continued to handle import and export business, with trains and wagons moved around by shunting engines, since the swing bridge over the Witham was not able to handle larger main-line locomotives.

The general principle of rail services in Lincolnshire seemed to be one of 'managed decline' with little investment forthcoming and a continuing erosion of what services there were. In October 1977, British Rail stopped the first and last trains to Skegness to save a staffing shift between there and Boston, although the decision was reversed later, but the capacity of trains on the route, especially on summer weekends, remains a source of concern to the South-East Lincolnshire Travellers' Association.

On the freight side, the trains on the Lincolnshire part of the old LD&ECR stopped in July 1980 and the final goods on the Louth-to-Grimsby section of the East Lincolnshire ran in December of the same year, although a passenger excursion between the towns did run before final closure. The track and trackbed were offered to the Grimsby-to-Louth Railway Preservation Society for £400,000, but they were not able to raise the necessary funds. The opening of the Humber Bridge in the summer of 1981 saw the end of the Humber ferries and the services to New Holland Town and Pier. Both stations closed, but a new New Holland halt was added to the Grimsby-to-Barton Line.

Excursions continued to be a valuable source of revenue to the railways, both into and out of the county. Deltic locomotive no. 55015 *Tulyar*

A class 31 leaves the Louth maltings on 18 March 1976. P.C. LOFTIS

Locomotives 50007 and COLAS 56096 approaching Ancaster with a steel train to Boston. 25 August 2010. GRAHAM LIGHTFOOT

Deltic no. 55015 Tulyar at Lincoln Central on 5 December 1981 with the Gainsborough Model Railway Society excursion 'The Hadrian Flyer' at Lincoln Central. The author is standing in the cab doorway.

hauled one trip to Skegness in August 1979, and an InterCity 125 High Speed Train ran from Grimsby to Edinburgh and the Forth Bridge later the same year and the Gainsborough Model Railways Society maintained its interest in special trips. They began when the Society was organizing enthusiasts' excursions to be hauled by the *Flying Scotsman* locomotive, bought for preservation by local businessman Alan Pegler. The author was privileged to ride the footplate of the *Flying Scotsman* on one such occasion and to get a cab trip in a Deltic on another.

The Spalding Flower Parade in May could always be guaranteed to draw large numbers of visitors, many of them travelling to the town in special excursion trains, with more than two dozen arriving and departing on the day during the late 1970s and early 1980s.

One Station for Lincoln

A major change to the county's rail infrastructure occurred on 11 May 1985 when all services to St Mark's station in Lincoln were diverted to Central station, and the St Mark's site sold for development as a retail site. To allow trains from Newark, including the through-London services, to enter Central station, the Lincoln Avoiding Line was closed and levelled with part of its route used by the new tracks. The Joint Line also suffered the closure, in November 1982, of the Spalding-to-March section, thus severing the alternative route from the north to London, and also of the Sleaford Avoiding Line. Parts of the former were sold off for development, but the latter remained *in situ*.

1985 also saw a proposal to close the Cleethorpes branch, and although that was not followed through, the track was singled between there and Grimsby. At the same time, the Cleethorpes-to-Newark loco-hauled trains were replaced by DMUs, resulting in complaints that not enough seats were available at peak times. The Cleethorpes-to-London HSTs were not affected by the change.

The trains themselves were also changing. In 1986, two-car class 155 Super Sprinters were introduced on the Newark–Lincoln route, but were not used in south Humberside, resulting in a need to change trains in Lincoln. The following year, the bus-based Pacers began to serve the Cleethorpes-to-Barton travellers. By 1990, it had become apparent that, for many routes, even the two-car 155s were more than were needed, and many were split to create single-unit class 153s, still common around the more rural parts of the county.

In 1989, another of Lincolnshire's earliest railways, that between Gainsborough and Grimsby, came under threat. British Rail announced that it would close the line, but it withdrew the idea two years later as it became apparent that it had value as a potential alternative goods route to the Humber

Class 37 locomotive with a mixed goods train on the Avoiding Line crossing the Lincoln–Newark tracks. Both lines were later removed when services were concentrated into Lincoln Central. PETER GREY COLLECTION, COURTESY OF LINCOLNSHIRE ARCHIVES

A pair of BR Regional Railways class 153s arrive at Wainfleet en route from Skegness to Crewe, 12 August 2003. ROD KNIGHT

ports. However, the passenger service was drastically cut back to the minimal level needed to avoid having to go through the process required to withdraw it completely. From October 1993, trains only ran on Saturdays: three in one direction and two in another!

Improvements to the Grimsby-to-Doncaster Line came about when Regional Railways extended the Cleethorpes-to-Sheffield service to Manchester and Manchester Airport in 1992, using the faster, quieter and more comfortable air-conditioned 158 Express Sprinters. However, Cleethorpes to Lincoln and beyond suffered a double blow when 153s were put onto the route to Newark, which became the only option for a London connection, as the through-HSTs were withdrawn on 16 May 1993. Goods services within the area, as opposed to the stream passing through to and from Immingham, had also been in decline, with Scunthorpe West, the last operational hump yard in the UK, closed and cleared for housing in 1990.

There was investment at Grimsby in 1993 when re-signalling took place over a month in the autumn of 1993, but even that had a sting in the tail, since Brocklesby and Elsham Stations closed the day after the lines were reopened in October.

A glimmer of the Good Old Days was glimpsed on 2 June 1995 when the Class 91 electric locomotive 91031 took a VIP train down *Mallard*'s old record racetrack on Stoke Bank, near Grantham, setting a new British speed record of 154mph (246km/h). Grantham was still Lincolnshire's showpiece for fast passenger services.

By the early 1990s, Lincolnshire's railways had settled into something of a rut – development where business was available, or where costs could be saved, but marking time at best on much of the network. A lot of campaigning was taking place, but mainly asking for more or better trains on existing lines, rather than looking for big new developments. An agreement was being worked on between British Rail and the county council in that the latter would help pay for the upgrading of parts of the Joint Line – reducing staffing by replacing manned level-crossings with automated barriers among other changes – in return for better passenger services between Doncaster and Peterborough by way of Gainsborough, Lincoln, Sleaford and Spalding. It was also expected that the agreement would see the opening of more new stations, with Donington and Pinchbeck earmarked as likely locations.

Nationally, however, major changes were afoot. In the run-up to the 1992 general election, the Conservative Government announced its intention to privatize British Rail if it was returned to power. At that time, it seemed an unlikely prospect, but the electorate surprised many by returning John Major – who had described British Rail as 'hopeless' – and his colleagues, and a new, and uncertain, world opened for the railways of Lincolnshire and the rest of the UK.

The plans were based on the view in the Conservative Party that a private operator would be intrinsically more efficient than a public one. That was not a universal opinion, even within the Party. An article in the *Independent* by Donald Macintyre quoted a colleague of the Great Privatizer, Margaret Thatcher, as saying she 'thought the railways were so bloody awful she wouldn't wish them on the private sector'. Despite coming from a railway town, Grantham, Mrs Thatcher never travelled by rail herself after becoming PM, nor did she propose selling them off, but her successor revived the idea.

How to Sell a Railway

A number of suggestions for the way that the sale might be achieved were put forward. Major favoured a return to something like the old Big Four – regional systems owning track, rolling stock and facilities – but this was not felt to offer the desired level of competitiveness. An alternative was put forward after the election by the new Transport Minister, John MacGregor, based, ironically, on a suggestion by the current popularizer of rail travel, Michael Portillo, then a junior minister in MacGregor's department.

Under their proposals, the tracks, stations and other fixed assets would remain in public

BRINGING BACK THE PAST

Two industrial locomotives at the Appleby Frodingham Railway Preservation Society base in Scunthorpe.

Preserved class 03 D2381 at Stainby sidings with Flying Scotsman's spare boiler being moved to Market Overton, July 1973. DAVID FORD

The railway preservation movement in the county got a boost in 1993 when the Great Northern and East Lincolnshire Railway Company bought the trackbed from Louth to Waltham and established a base at Ludborough. They had been given authorization to 'run a railway for not more than 10½ miles' the previous year, but hopes that they might eventually connect with the national network at Grimsby were dashed by the local authority's use of the northern section for the new Peake's Parkway road. A couple of years earlier, the Appleby Frodingham Railway Preservation Society had formed to preserve railway equipment in the steelworks at Scunthorpe. The society owned locomotives and rolling stock, but made use of the tracks that served the works.

In the south of the county, and just over the border into neighbouring Rutland, the High Dyke mining branch had been the scene of an attempt in the early 1970s to set up a railway heritage centre, with *Flying Scotsman* and *Pendennis Castle* stabled there for a while. The project did not take off, but Rocks by Rail, formerly known as the Rutland Railway Museum, is operating in the area, using restored iron ore working equipment and other relevant material.

Two smaller lines in the north of the county continue the traditions of a seaside railway. The Cleethorpes Coast Light Railway is a 15in gauge line running for about 2 miles (3km) along the seafront built by the borough council in 1948. The line is now privately owned and was extended and upgraded in 2007. Cleethorpes, or more exactly, the village of Humberston, was served by the Lincolnshire Coast Light Railway, which operated from 1960 to 1985, carrying holidaymakers from a bus terminus

to the beach and to the Fitties – an area developed in the 1920s by people wanting to build their own homes by the sea. The LCLR was laid using material from the Nocton potato railway, which, in turn, made use of material from World War One military lines. After closing at Humberston, some of the equipment was stored until a new site was found at the Ingoldmells Water Leisure Park near Skegness. The line there opened on 3 May 2009.

Jurassic at Beach station on the Cleethorpes Coast Light Railway. ALAN TYE

ownership for the time being, but the actual train services would be franchised out to private train operating companies (TOCs). A number of fixed franchises were set out, with parts of Lincolnshire being served by three passenger and four freight sectors. These would be auctioned off to whoever offered a combination of the best service and the highest return or lowest amount of subsidy, depending on the traffic expected. There would also be an 'open access' option on a limited number of routes for other private operators wanting to compete with the franchisees. Rolling stock was to be owned by rolling stock operating companies (ROSCOs).

There was considerable concern about the plans within Lincolnshire, as well as nationally. A Lincolnshire County Council report in 1995 described the future of rail use to be 'uncertain', arguing that the government's position that rail use would rise 'due to the responsiveness of the private sector to market demand' had not been proven, and that a further decline was equally possible:

> If there are lines or services which are not profitable, then, as with bus deregulation, there is likely to be pressure to close them. Rail privatisation is therefore a matter of great concern to the County, since any further reduction in the depth of rail services will further reduce the availability of alternatives to car transport.

Parliamentary opposition was led by the all-party Commons Transport Select Committee. A report produced under the chairmanship of Tory MP Robert Adley said privatization could destroy the railways, but the unfortunate death of Mr Adley at a crucial moment destroyed its momentum.

The final proposals were put to Parliament as the Railways Act 1993, implemented in April 1994. British Rail then restructured its business model to match the proposed new model. Passenger services were divided into twenty-five different train-operating units and run as 'shadow' businesses paying access charges for the use of track and infrastructure, and rentals for stations and rolling stock.

Private Transport – by Rail and Bus!

It took a little while for the process of franchising to get under way, but the first privately operated trains for nearly half a century reached Lincolnshire in April 1994 when GNER – Great North Eastern Railway – began to serve Grantham as part of its East Coast franchise. It also served Lincoln, but indirectly, with a bus service from there to Newark to connect with its trains. The remaining passenger services in the county moved in 1997 to National Express, operating the Central Trains franchise covering most of the county except for the Sheffield to Lincoln and Grimsby to Gainsborough and Doncaster routes. These became part of the Arriva Trains Northern franchise, operated from 1998 as Northern Spirit.

The new structure led to the dropping of many of the plans for improvement developed by LCC and British Rail. Local RDS campaigner Paul Jowett described the period as 'limbo land':

> 1996 should have seen Sleaford–Spalding modernized and Donington and Pinchbeck stations opened, and an hourly service from Doncaster to Lincoln and Peterborough. Sadly we seem as far away as ever from these real improvements. In fact there have been cuts, by 50 per cent in the case of the Lincoln–Doncaster service. The changes have wrecked many chances of connections.

At least one rather surprising connection that became available in 1998 was a Skegness-to-Cardiff service operated by Central Trains. It can hardly have been the most comfortable trip on a DMU.

The government's desire to see more competition in rail services was thwarted on the goods side in 1995 and 1996, when North and South Railways, a consortium set up by the American Wisconsin Central Railway Company, bought up most of the rail freight franchises and organized them into a new company, English Welsh and Scottish Railway Ltd (EWSR). This amalgamation was accepted by the authorities on the grounds that rail freight

EWS class 56 no. 56094 at Barnetby with coal for Scunthorpe, 26 July 2000. DAVID FORD

already faced strong competition from road-haulage operators. New operators have since emerged to compete with EWSR and its successors. A local benefit was seen as Boston Dock was reconnected to the national network in 1997 on the completion of the new Boston Rail Terminal. The connection had been severed in 1993. Steel coil is now imported through Boston Docks with trains using the lines through Sleaford to Grantham and beyond.

The development of railways in Lincolnshire in the past two decades has been mainly a matter of investment into goods facilities and some more or less gentle reshuffling of passenger services and their operating companies.

One-Fifth of Britain's Goods by Rail

On the goods side, the focus has been on improving the services in and out of the Immingham port complex, which now handles around a fifth of total UK rail freight. According to one enthusiasts' website, Barnetby, at the junction of the lines serving Lincoln, Gainsborough and Doncaster, is believed to be the busiest station in Britain for goods, typically seeing something like 150 freights pass through in a 24-hour day. Over 30 of those are iron ore trains and about 60 carry coal or biomass – half-loaded and half of them empty in each case. A further 16 serve the steel industry; a couple of dozen oil trains pass to and from the refinery complexes, and other movements include chemicals, new cars, coke, scrap metal and departmental traffic. It is estimated that this adds up to a quarter of a million tonnes of freight passing through every day.

Traffic into the area that doesn't get as far as Barnetby includes occasional coal trains from South Wales and two trains of slab steel to Scotland and the north-east, plus one to France by way of the Channel Tunnel. The so-called 'bin-liner trains' carry landfill material from the Manchester area to a site at Roxby, north of Scunthorpe, on part of old NLLR. To facilitate the movement of much of this traffic, the Doncaster North Chord opened recently, creating what is effectively a rail by-pass around the town to avoid delays caused by goods trains from Immingham and north Lincolnshire using or crossing the ECML. The Freight on Rail Partnership, an industry campaign body, would like new links to be built within the Immingham complex, as well as work on the lines to allow an increase in goods train speeds up to 60 or 75mph (96 or 120km/h).

In 2008, Network Rail announced plans to upgrade what remains of the Joint Line and the southern Lincolnshire Loop to take goods traffic off the ECML, and this work is going on at the time of writing. Re-signalling of the Lincoln area has taken place, with the clusters of semaphore signals and the signal boxes that controlled them vanishing to be replaced by coloured lights operated from Doncaster. As part of the Joint Line upgrade, another twenty-four signal and gate boxes were replaced in 2013–14 along with most of the gates at level-crossings. The improvements also required modifications to bridges and level-crossings in Lincoln, to mitigate the return of significant delays to town traffic caused by the increasing number of trains crossing the High Street.

On the passenger side, GNER saw its franchise renewed, but, following the collapse of parent company Sea Containers in 2006, it gave up the business, which was taken on by National Express the following year. As part of their bid, they promised to bring back direct Lincoln-to-London services, but defaulted on the whole franchise in 2009. It was taken back in hand by the government-owned Directly Operated Railways, trading as East Coast, but they reduced the Lincoln commitment from a two-hourly service to one train a day each way. The franchise has now been taken up by Virgin Trains/Stagecoach combinations who have agreed to increase the Lincoln service frequency by 2019.

In the north of the county, 2004 saw Northern Spirit mutate into TransPennine Express, then later into Northern Rail, with few changes other

Oil trains in north Lincolnshire. ABOVE: Britannia 70036 passes Appleby box and station in July 1962 (JOHN FOREMAN). BELOW: DBS 66063 near Melton Ross, 28 February 2014 (GRAHAM LIGHTFOOT). Both trains heading west.

than the introduction of class 185 Desiro units. The rough-riding Pacers remain in service, with the possibility that they may be internally upgraded, but without much reduction in vibration. A suggested alternative is that refurbished London Underground trains might be introduced in the

Class 185 Desiro units waiting in Scunthorpe station, September 2014.

East Midlands Trains class 156 leaving Lincoln Central over the notorious High Street level crossing, 12 July 2008. GRAHAM LIGHTFOOT

area. The prospect has not been greeted with enthusiasm.

Central Trains was disbanded in 2007, with their services taken over by an expanded East Midlands franchise, who promised, and introduced, a Lincoln–London HST service. Unfortunately for travellers, the new facility ran by way of Nottingham and the Midland Main Line, meaning that it was still usually quicker to travel to Newark and change there for the ECML. One tiny part of the county did see a return of rail services in 2009, however, when the Lincolnshire Wolds Railway opened its second station, at North Thoresby. It thereby gained a small financial benefit in that, as a railway with more than one station, it did not have to add value added tax to its ticket prices!

The continuing struggle of most rail-passenger services in the county was emphasized in 2011 when the McNulty Report recommended closing ticket offices at Boston, Skegness, Sleaford, Spalding and Stamford, and reducing them at Cleethorpes, Grimsby and Scunthorpe to save money.

Crystal Ball Time

With Lincolnshire's railways approaching their 170th birthday in 2016, what does the future hold for what is left of the once county-wide network? On goods the answer would appear to be clear – a continuing development and improvement of

Peckett 0–4–0 Fulstow no. 2 prepares to take a train away from the Lincolnshire Wolds Railway base at Ludborough.

services to and from Scunthorpe and Immingham, and the increasing use of the Joint Line as a freight artery between the north and south – exactly what it was built for a century and a half ago. Will the 'missing link' between Spalding and March ever be restored? It would be enormously valuable, but also enormously expensive. A major switch to freight by rail would certainly justify that, and the proposed development of a rail hub for food distribution in the Spalding area would increase the benefits of a more direct link to the East Anglian ports of Harwich and Felixstowe. Closing the gap would also offer the option of a passenger service into East Anglia – perhaps even a direct Lincoln–London service by way of Cambridge, finally completing the earliest rail proposals for the county!

More achievable passenger options making use of the upgrade on the Joint Line would be an improved Doncaster–Lincoln–Sleaford–Spalding–Peterborough service offering better in-county and longer-distance connections.

David Harby, Railfuture Lincolnshire Branch Chairman, has such possibilities at the top of the organization's 'wish list' for the county. He envisages electrification for the route, claiming that the freight operators for which it is intended are reluctant to invest in electric locomotives until all main goods routes are electrified. With that in mind, he suggests that a useful passenger service might start at Leeds before running onto the Joint Line at Doncaster and continuing as above. The long-planned station at Donington could then be added, as might another at Finningley, to serve Robin Hood Airport. Proposed housing and other developments at Gainsborough, giving it formal Growth Point status, should help to finance a new station at Lea Road.

Gainsborough would also benefit by the restoration of more normal services to Brigg and Grimsby, but David expects those to come as a result of improvements in the whole route from Sheffield by way of Worksop and Retford, where congestion is already a problem. Increasing numbers of goods trains on the line as lighter bulk biomass replaces some coal trains – three wood-chip equals two coal,

East Midlands class 153 rejoining the Joint Line at Sleaford North on its way to Lincoln, 5 September 2102. RAY HEPPENSTALL

apparently – could require the redoubling of the tracks.

On the other ex-GCR lines, he echoed the freight group's call for increased speeds on the Grimsby-to-Doncaster route, as well as an hourly service between Lincoln and Grimsby. A new station at Cherry Willingham could be added, but that would be 'a non-starter' without the increased frequency.

A dream project would be the electrification of the Lincoln-to-Nottingham Line, but for the moment he would settle for two trains per hour

The problems of partial electrification. Diesel loco 67022 hauls East Coast electric 91109 and a Leeds to King's Cross train past the old Stow Park station on the Joint Line during a diversion from the ECML. 8 June 2013. GRAHAM LIGHTFOOT

between the cities, with one stopping only at Newark and the other all-stations; but he expects major improvements to have to wait for the Newark Flyover, expected some time around 2020.

His final call is for better Skegness services on winter Sundays, which don't currently start until around 1400, but he accepts that will probably have to wait for re-signalling some time in the next 10–15 years.

If we return to the opening paragraph of this book, it is ironic that even after the coming and near departure of the railways, communications in Lincolnshire are still a matter of ancient routes often clogged with slow-moving goods vehicles, while our towns are full of people in cars looking for parking places. Even our over-pruned railway system could be doing a lot more to ease some of those pressures, but insufficient investment, that

long-term bane of railway development, looks likely to continue into the immediate future at the least. What funds are available, are probably better spent on the kind of project that delivers national and regional benefit, such as HS2 and the Northern Hub, which might just spin off some goodies for Lincolnshire. But major spending on a network originally built largely to serve local travellers, traders and farmers would be unlikely to generate significant economic growth.

We look like having to live with what we have got, at least for the time being, but we do need to support the watchdogs of Railfuture, SELTA, the Friends of the Barton Line and of the Brigg and Lincoln Lines, the Market Rasen Rail Users Group and all the others who keep an eye on this important part of Lincolnshire's transport network. The railways have worked for Lincolnshire, and they can do it again.

Visions of the future? A class 68, the newest locomotive type in Britain at the time of writing, hauling a train over the upgraded Joint Line through the reopened station at Metheringham. MICHAEL EPPINGER

Railway Abbreviations

AJR	Axholme Joint Railway
AN&B&EJR	Ambergate, Nottingham and Boston and Eastern Junction Railway
BR	British Railways or British Rail
BS&MCR	Boston, Sleaford and Midland Counties Railway
BTC	British Transport Commission
E&M	Eastern and Midlands Railway
EC	Eastern Counties
ECML	East Coast Main Line – the GNR Towns Line
ELR	East Lincolnshire Railway
EWSR	English Welsh and Scottish Railway
G&MLR	Goole and Marshland Light Railway
GCR	Great Central Railway
GER	Great Eastern Railway
GG&SJR	Great Grimsby and Sheffield Junction Railway
GNR	Great Northern Railway
IoALR	Isle of Axholme Light Railway
L&LR	Louth and Lincoln Railway
L&SB	Lynn & Sutton Bridge
L&YR	Lancashire and Yorkshire Railway
LD&ECR	Lancashire, Derbyshire and East Coast Railway
LMSR	London, Midland and Scottish Railway
LNER	London and North Eastern Railway
M&GNR	Midland and Great Northern Joint Railway
MR	Midland Railway
MS&LR	Manchester, Sheffield and Lincolnshire Railway
N&SR	Norwich and Spalding Railway
NER	North Eastern Railway
NLLR	North Lindsey Light Railway
RDS	Railway Development Society
S&FR	Spilsby and Firsby Railway
S&LJR	Sheffield & Lincolnshire Junction
S&W	Sutton and Willoughby Railway
SELTA	South-East Lincolnshire Travellers' Association
SYR	South Yorkshire Railway
TA&GR	Trent, Ancholme and Grimsby Railway
W&FR	Wainfleet and Firsby Railway
WL&BR	Wakefield, Lincoln and Boston Railway

Bibliography

Allen, C. J., *The London & North Eastern Railway* (Ian Allan, 1986)

Anderson, P., *Railways of Lincolnshire* (Irwell Press, 1992)

Bates, C. and Bairstow, M., *Railways in North Lincolnshire* (Martin Bairstow, 2005)

Body, G., *The Railway Era* (Moorland, 1982)

Bonavia, M., *A History of the LNER, Vols 1–3* (George Allen & Unwin, 1983)

Cupit, J. and Taylor, W., *The Lancashire, Derbyshire and East Coast Railway* (Oakwood, 1988)

Dow, G., *Great Central, Vols 1–3* (The Locomotive Publishing Company, 1959)

Engel, M., *Eleven Minutes Late* (Macmillan, 2009)

Franks, D. L., *The Stamford & Essendine Railway* (Turntable Enterprises, 1971)

Goode, C. T., *The Railways of North Lincolnshire* (C. T. Goode, 1985)

Goode, C. T., *The Great Northern & Great Eastern Joint Railway* (C. T. Goode, 1989)

Gordon, W. J., *Our Home Railways, Vol 2* (Frederick Warne, 1910)

Grinling, C. H., *The History of the Great Northern Railway, 1898* (Reprinted by George Allen & Unwin, 1966)

Hemingway, G., (Compilation) *Source Material of the Great Northern Railway* (GNRS, 2000)

Jackson, D. and Russell, O., *The Great Central in LNER Days 2* (Ian Allan, 1986)

King, P. K. and Hewins, D. R., *The Railways around Grimsby, Cleethorpes, Immingham and NE Lincs* (Foxline Publishing, 1988)

Ludlam, A. J., *The Spilsby to Firsby Railway* (Oakwood, 1985)

Ludlam, A. J., *The Horncastle and Woodhall Junction Railway* (Oakwood, 1986)

Ludlam, A. J., *The Louth, Mablethorpe and Willoughby Loop* (Oakwood, 1987)

Ludlam, A. J., *The East Lincolnshire Railway* (Oakwood, 1991)

Ludlam, A. J., *The Lincolnshire Loop Line (GNR) and the River Witham* (Oakwood, 1995)

Ludlam, A. J., *Railways to New Holland and the Humber Ferries* (Oakwood, 1996)

Ludlam, A. J., *Railways to Skegness* (Oakwood, 1997)

Ludlam, A. J. and Herbert, W. B., *The Louth to Bardney Branch* (Oakwood, 1984)

May, T., *The Victorian Railway Worker* (Shire Books, 2000)

Oates, G., *The Axholme Joint Railway* (Oakwood Press, 1961)

Pearson, R. E. and Ruddock, J. G., *Lord Willoughby's Railway* (Willoughby Memorial Trust, 1986)

Rhodes, J., *Bourne to Essendine* (KMS Books, 1986)

Rhodes, J., *Great Northern Branch Lines to Stamford* (KMS Books, 1988)

Rhodes, J., *Bourne to Saxby* (KMS Books, 1989)

Ruddock, J. G. and Pearson, R. E., *The Railway History of Lincoln* (J. Ruddock Ltd, 1985)

Squires, S. E., *The Lincolnshire Potato Railways* (Oakwood, 1987)

Squires, S. E., *The Lost Railways of Lincolnshire* (Castlemead, 1988)

Squires, S. E., *The Lincoln to Grantham Line via Honington* (Oakwood, 1996)

Squires, S. E. and Hollamby, K., *Building a Railway Bourne to Saxby* (Lincolnshire Record Society, 2009)

Stennett, A., *The Lost Railways of Lincolnshire* (Countryside, 2007)

Walker, S., *Great Northern Branch Lines in Lincolnshire* (KMS Books, 1984)

Walker, S., *The New Line: Kirkstead–Little Steeping* (KMS Books, 1985)

Walker, S., *Great Central Branch Lines in Lincolnshire* (KMS Books, 1986)

Walker, S., *Firsby to Wainfleet and Skegness* (KMS Books, 1987)

Walter, J. C., *A History of Horncastle from the Earliest Period to the Present Time* (W. K. Morton & Sons, 1908)

Wright, N., *Lincolnshire Towns and Industry 1700–1914* (History of Lincolnshire Committee, 1982)

Wrottesley, A. J., *The Midland & Great Northern Joint Railway* (David & Charles, 1970)

Wrottesley, A. J., *The Great Northern Railway, Vols 1–3* (Batsford, 1979)

Also: the magazines of the Great Northern Railway Society, the Lincolnshire Wolds Railway Society, the Lincoln Railway Society, and the Lincolnshire and East Yorkshire Transport Review.

Index